Pascal User Manual and Report

Kathleen Jensen
Niklaus Wirth

Pascal User Manual and Report

Revised for the ISO Pascal Standard

Third Edition, Prepared by
Andrew B. Mickel
James F. Miner

Springer-Verlag
New York Berlin Heidelberg Tokyo

Kathleen Jensen
Digital Equipment Corporation
Educational Services
Bedford, MA 01730
U.S.A.

Niklaus Wirth
Institute für Informatik
ETH-Zentrum
CH-8092 Zürich
Switzerland

Andrew B. Mickel
Apollo Computer
Minneapolis, MN 55435
U.S.A.

James F. Miner
University Computer Center
University of Minnesota
Minneapolis, MN 55455
U.S.A.

AMS Subject Classifications (1983):68-02, 68A05, 68B99
CR Subject Classification (1983): D.2.1, D.3.2

Library of Congress Cataloging in Publication Data
Jensen,Kathleen
    Pascal: user manual and report
    Bibliography: p.
    Includes index.
    1. Pascal (Computer program language) I. Wirth,
Niklaus. II. Mickel, Andrew B. III. Miner, James F.
IV. Title.
QA76.73.P2J46 1985   001.64'24   84—10615

With 76 Illustrations.

Illustrations by William W. Porter.
Typeset by Human Factors, Inc., Leverett, Massachusetts.
Printed and bound by R.R. Donnelley & Sons, Harrisonburg, Virginia.
Printed in the United States of America.

9 8 7 6 5 4 3 2 1

ISBN 0-387-96048-1 Springer-Verlag New York Berlin Heidelberg Tokyo
ISBN 3-540-96048-1 Springer-Verlag Berlin Heidelberg New York Tokyo

Foreword

For nearly a decade *Pascal User Manual and Report* has served as the standard tutorial and reference book for practicing programmers who wanted to learn and use Pascal. During the 1970's the popularity of Pascal grew beyond anyone's expectations and has become one of the most important computer programming languages used throughout the world. At that time in the United States, commercial use of Pascal often exceeded academic interest. Today most universities use Pascal to teach programming. Pascal is the modern alternative to PL/1 or Algol 60, and even Fortran is changing to take advantage of Pascal's innovations.

In our work with Pascal User's Group and *Pascal News,* we witnessed the spread of Pascal implementations to every modern computer system. In 1971 one computer system had a Pascal compiler. By 1974 the number had grown to 10 and in 1979 there were more than 80. Pascal is always available on those ubiquitous breeds of computer systems: personal computers and professional workstations.

Questions arising out of the Southampton Symposium on Pascal in 1977 [Reference 10] began the first organized effort to write an officially sanctioned, international Pascal Standard. Participants sought to consolidate the list of questions that naturally arose when people tried to implement Pascal compilers using definitions found in the *Pascal User Manual and Report.* That effort culminated in the ISO 7185 Pascal Standard [Reference 11] which officially defines Pascal and necessitated the revision of this book.

We have chosen to modify the User Manual and the Report with respect to the Standard – not to make this book a substitute for the

v

Standard. As a result this book retains much of its readability and elegance which, we believe, set it apart from the Standard. We updated the syntactic notation to Niklaus Wirth's EBNF and improved the style of programs in the User Manual. For the convenience of readers familiar with previous editions of this book, we have included Appendix E which summarizes the changes necessitated by the Standard.

Finally, there ought to be a note in this book that Pascal was named after the French mathematician, humanist, and religious fanatic Blaise Pascal, who built a simple calculating machine. We wish to thank Roberto Minio and Niklaus Wirth for their support of the project to revise this book. Henry Ledgard offered us much timely and consistently useful advice. Elise Oranges conscientiously facilitated production schedules. We also thank William W. Porter for his artwork and Linda Strzegowski who did the typesetting for this edition.

Andy Mickel
Jim Miner
Minneapolis, USA
November, 1984

Preface

A preliminary version of the programming language Pascal was drafted
in 1968. It followed in its spirit the Algol 60 and Algol W line of
languages. After an extensive development phase, a first compiler
became operational in 1970, and publication followed a year later [see
References 1 and 8.] The growing interest in the development of
compilers for other computers called for a consolidation of Pascal,
and two years of experience in the use of the language dictated a few
revisions. This led in 1973 to the publication of a Revised Report and
a definition of a language representation in terms of the ISO character
set.

    This book consists of two parts: The User Manual, and the
Revised Report. The *User Manual* is directed to those who have
previously acquired some familiarity with computer programming,
and who wish to get acquainted with the language Pascal. Hence, the
style of the User Manual is that of a tutorial, and many examples are
included to demonstrate the various features of Pascal. Summarizing
tables and syntax specifications are added as Appendices. The *Report*
is included in this book to serve as a concise, ultimate reference for
both programmers and implementors. It describes Standard Pascal
which constitutes a common base between various implementations
of the language.

    The linear structure of a book is by no means ideal for introducing
a language. Nevertheless, in its use as a tutorial, we recommend
following the given organization of the User Manual, paying careful
attention to the example programs, and then to reread those sections

which cause difficulties. In particular, one may wish to reference Chapter 12, if questions arise concerning input and output conventions.

Chapter 0-12 of the User Manual, and the entire Report, describe Standard Pascal. Implementors should regard the task of recognizing ISO Standard Pascal as the basic requirement of their systems, whereas programmers who intend their programs to be transportable from one computer system to another should use only features described as Standard Pascal. Of course, individual implementations may provide additional facilities which, however, should be clearly labelled as extensions.

The efforts of many go into the User Manual, and we especially thank the members of the Institut fuer Informatik, ETH Zurich, and John Larmouth, Rudy Schild, Olivier Lecarme, and Pierre Desjardins for their criticism, suggestions, and encouragement. Our implementation of Pascal—which made this manual both possible and necessary — is the work of Urs Ammann, aided by Helmut Sandmayr.

Kathleen Jensen
Niklaus Wirth
ETH Zurich
Switzerland
November, 1974

Table of Contents

USER MANUAL (Pascal Tutorial) by K. Jensen and N. Wirth

REPORT (Pascal Reference) by N. Wirth

List of Figures

USER MANUAL

CHAPTER 0

Introduction

0.A.   An Overview of Pascal Programs

Much of the following text assumes that you, the reader, have a minimal grasp of computer terminology and a "feeling" for the structure of a program. The purpose of this section is to spark your intuition.

An *algorithm* or computer program consists of two essential parts, a description of *actions* that are to be performed, and a description of the *data,* that are manipulated by these actions. Actions are described by so-called *statements,* and data are described by so-called *declarations* and *definitions.*

The program is divided into a *heading* and a body, called a *block.* The heading gives the program a name and lists its parameters. These are (file) variables and represent the arguments and results of the computation. The block consists of six sections, where any except the last may be empty. They must appear in the order given in the definition for a block:

> *Block* = *LabelDeclarationPart*
> *ConstantDefinitionPart*
> *TypeDefinitionPart*
> *VariableDeclarationPart*
> *ProcedureAndFunctionDeclarationPart*
> *StatementPart* .

1

An Example Program

```
program Inflation(Output);

   { Assuming annual inflation rates of 7%, 8%, and 10%,
     find the factor by which any unit of currency such as
     the franc, dollar, pound sterling, mark, ruble, yen, or
     guilder will have been devalued in 1, 2, ..., n years. }

   const
     MaxYears = 10;

   var
     Year: 0..MaxYears;
     Factor1, Factor2, Factor3: Real;

begin
   Year := 0;
   Factor1 := 1.0;  Factor2 := 1.0;  Factor3 := 1.0;
   Writeln(' Year      7%     8%    10%'); Writeln;
   repeat
     Year := Year + 1;
     Factor1 := Factor1 * 1.07;
     Factor2 := Factor2 * 1.08;
     Factor3 := Factor3 * 1.10;
     Writeln(Year :5, Factor1 :7:3, Factor2 :7:3, Factor3 :7:3)
   until Year = MaxYears
end .
```

Produces as results:

Year	7%	8%	10%
1	1.070	1.080	1.100
2	1.145	1.166	1.210
3	1.225	1.260	1.331
4	1.311	1.360	1.464
5	1.403	1.469	1.611
6	1.501	1.587	1.772
7	1.606	1.714	1.949
8	1.718	1.851	2.144
9	1.838	1.999	2.358
10	1.967	2.159	2.594

The first section lists all labels defined in this block. The second section defines synonyms for constants; i.e., it introduces "constant identifiers" that may later be used in place of those constants. The third contains type definitions; and the fourth, variable definitions. The fifth section defines subordinate program parts (i.e., procedures and functions). The statement part specifies the actions to be taken.

0.B.   Syntax Diagrams

The previous program outline is more graphically expressed in a *syntax diagram*. Starting at the diagram for *Program* (Figure 0.a), a path through the diagram defines a syntactically correct program. Each rectangular box references a diagram by that name, which is then used to define its meaning. Terminal symbols (those actually written in a Pascal program) are in rounded enclosures. (See Appendix D for the complete set of diagrams for Pascal.)

0.C.   EBNF

An alternative method for describing syntax is the *Extended Backus-Naur Form*, (EBNF), where syntactic constructs are denoted by English words and literals. These words are suggestive of the nature or meaning of the construct while the literals denote actual symbols used in writing the language. Literals are enclosed in quotation marks.

Enclosure of a sequence of constructs and literals by the meta-symbols { and } implies its occurrence zero or more times. Alternatives are separated by the metasymbol | . Parentheses (and) are used for grouping and the metasymbols [and] denote that the enclosed constructs and literals are optional. (A complete explanation of EBNF and the EBNF of Pascal is given in Appendix D.) As an example, the construct *Program* of Figure 0.a is defined by the following EBNF formulas called *productions*.

```
Program          =  ProgramHeading ";"  Block ".".
ProgramHeading   =  "program" Identifier ["(" IdentifierList ")"].
IdentifierList   =  Identifier {"," Identifier}.
```

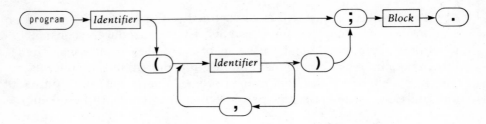

Figure 0.a   Syntax diagram for *Program*

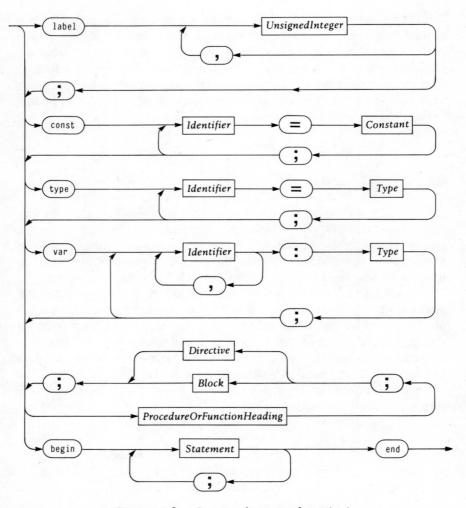

Figure 0.b   Syntax diagram for *Block*

0.D. Scope

Each procedure and function declaration has a structure similar to a program; i.e., each consists of a heading and a block. Hence, procedure and function declarations may be nested within other procedures or functions. Labels, constant synonyms, type, variable, procedure, and function declarations are *local* to the procedure or function in which they are declared. That is, their identifiers have significance only within the program text that constitutes the block. This region of program text is called the *scope* of these identifiers. Since blocks may be nested, so may scopes. Objects that are declared in the main program, i.e., not local to some procedure or function, are called *global* and have significance throughout the entire program.

Since blocks may be nested within other blocks by procedure and function declarations, one is able to assign a level of nesting to each. If the outermost program-defined block (e.g., the main program) is called level 0, then a block defined within this block would be of level 1; in general, a block defined in level i would be of level (i+1). Figure 0.c illustrates a block structure.

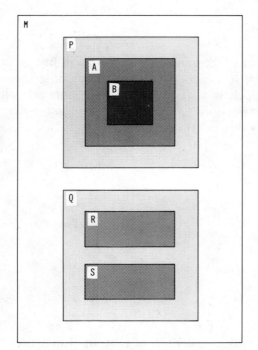

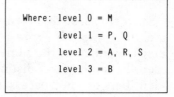

```
Where: level 0 = M
       level 1 = P, Q
       level 2 = A, R, S
       level 3 = B
```

Figure 0.c   Block structure

This block structure could represent the following program skeleton:

```
program M;
   procedure P;
      procedure A;
         procedure B;
         begin
         end { B };
      begin
      end { A };
   begin
   end { P };
   procedure Q;
      procedure R;
      begin
      end { R };
      procedure S;
      begin
      end { S };
   begin
   end { Q };
begin
end { M }.
```

In terms of this formulation the scope or range of validity of an identifier X is the entire block in which X is defined, including those blocks defined in the same block as X. (For this example, note that all identifiers must be distinct. Section 3.G discusses the case where identifiers are not necessarily distinct.)

block	may access objects in blocks
M	M
P	P, M
A	A, P, M
B	B, A, P, M
Q	Q, M
R	R, Q, M
S	S, Q, M

0.E. Miscellaneous

For programmers acquainted with Algol, PL/I, or Fortran, it may prove helpful to glance at Pascal in terms of these other languages. For this purpose, we list the following characteristics of Pascal:

1. Declaration of variables is mandatory.

2. Certain key words (e.g., begin, end, repeat) are "reserved" and cannot be used as identifiers.

3. The semicolon (;) is considered as a statement separator.

4. The standard data types are those of whole and real numbers, the logical values, and the (printable) characters. The basic data structuring facilities include the array, the record (corresponding to Cobol's and PL/I's "structure"), the set, and the (sequential) file. These structures can be combined and nested to form arrays of sets, files of records, etc. Data may be allocated dynamically and accessed via pointers. These pointers allow the full generality of list processing. There is a facility to declare new, basic data
types with symbolic constants.

5. The set data structure offers facilities similar to the PL/I "bit string".

6. Arrays may be of arbitrary dimension with arbitrary bounds; the array bounds are constant (i.e., there are no dynamic arrays.)

7. As in Fortran, Algol, and PL/I, there is a goto statement. Labels are unsigned integers and must be declared.

8. The compound statement is that of Algol, and corresponds to the DO group in PL/I.

9. The facilities of the Algol switch and the computed goto of Fortran are represented by the case statement.

10. The for statement, corresponding to the DO loop of Fortran, may only have steps of 1 (to) or −1 (downto) and is executed only as long as the value of the control variable lies within the limits. Consequently, the controlled statement may not be executed at all.

11. There are no conditional expressions and no multiple assignments.

12. Procedures and functions may be called recursively.

13. There is no "own" attribute for variables (as in Algol).

14. Parameters are passed either by value or by reference; there is no "call by name."

15. The "block structure" differs from that of Algol and PL/I insofar as there are no anonymous blocks; i.e., each block is given a name and thereby is made into a procedure or function.

16. All objects — constants, variables, etc. — must be declared *before* they are referenced. The following two exceptions are however allowed:
    a. the type identifier in a pointer type definition (Chapter 10)
    b. procedure and function identifiers when there is a forward declaration (Section 11.C).

Upon first contact with Pascal, some programmers tend to bemoan the absence of certain "favorite features." Examples include an exponentiation operator, concatenation of strings, dynamic arrays, arithmetic operations on Boolean values, automatic type conversions, and default declarations. These were not oversights, but deliberate omissions. In some cases their presence would be primarily an invitation to inefficient programming solutions; in others, it was felt that they would be contrary to the aim of clarity and reliability and "good programming style." Finally, a rigorous selection among the immense variety of programming facilities available had to be made in order to keep Pascal compilers relatively compact and efficient — efficient and economical for both the user who writes only small programs using few constructs of the language and the user who writes large programs and tends to make use of the full language.

CHAPTER 1

Notation: Symbols and Separators

Pascal programs are represented by symbols and symbol separators. Pascal symbols include *special symbols, word symbols,* identifiers, numbers, character strings, labels, and directives. *Symbol separators* are explained in the next section.

1.A.   Separators

Blanks, ends-of-lines (line separators), and comments are considered as symbol separators. No part of a separator can occur within a Pascal symbol. You must use at least one separator between two consecutive identifiers, word-symbols, or numbers.

A *comment* begins with either { or (* (not inside a character string) and ends with either a } or *). A comment may contain any sequence of end-of-lines and characters except } or *). A comment may be replaced with a space in the program text without altering its meaning.

Often you can improve the readability of a Pascal program by inserting blanks, end-of-lines (blank lines), and comments in it.

1.B.   Special Symbols and Word Symbols

Here is a list of the special symbols and word symbols used to write
Pascal programs. Note that two-character special symbols are written
without any intervening separators. Here are the special symbols:

```
+    -    *    /
.    ,    :    ;
=    <>   <    <=   >    >=
:=   ..   ↑
(    )    [    ]
```

Alternative special symbols:

```
(.          for  [
.)          for  ]
@ or  ^     for  ↑
```

   Word symbols (or reserved words) are normally underlined in the
hand-written program to emphasize their interpretation as single
symbols with fixed meaning. You may not use these words in a
context other than that explicit in the definition of Pascal: in particular, these words may not be used as identifiers. They are written as a
sequence of upper-case or lower-case letters (without surrounding
escape characters). Here are the word-symbols:

and	end	nil	set
array	file	not	then
begin	for	of	to
case	function	or	type
const	goto	packed	until
div	if	procedure	var
do	in	program	while
downto	label	record	with
else	mod	repeat	

1.C.   Identifiers

Identifiers are names denoting constants, types, bounds, variables,
procedures, and functions. They must begin with a letter, which may
be followed by any combination and number of letters and digits. The
spelling of an identifier is significant over its whole length. Corresponding upper-case and lower-case letters are considered equivalent.

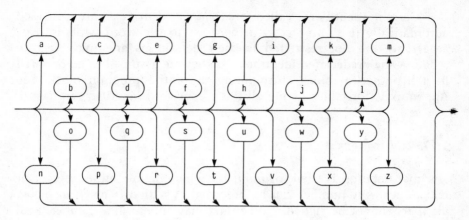

Figure 1.a Syntax diagram for *Letter*

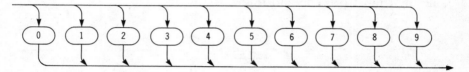

Figure 1.b Syntax diagram for *Digit*

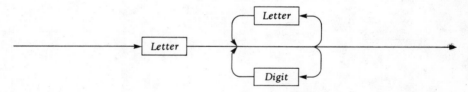

Figure 1.c Syntax diagram for *Identifier*

Examples of identifiers:
```
PhoneList   Root3   Pi   h4g   X
ThisIsAVeryLongButNeverTheLessValidIdentifier
ThisIsAVeryLongButDifferentIdentifierThanTheOneAbove
```

LettersAndDigits denotes the same identifier as lettersanddigits.

These are not identifiers:

```
3rd    array    level.4    Root-3    Tenth_Planet
```

Certain identifiers, called *predeclared identifiers,* are provided automatically (e.g., sin, cos). In contrast to the word-symbols (e.g., array), we are not restricted to their definitions and may elect to redefine any predeclared identifiers, as they are assumed to be declared in a hypothetical block surrounding the entire program block. See Appendix C for tables listing all the predeclared identifiers in Pascal.

1.D.   Numbers

Decimal notation is used for *numbers,* which denote either integer or real values. Any number can be preceded by a sign (+ or –); *unsigned numbers* cannot be signed. No comma may appear in a number. Real numbers are written with a decimal or scale factor or both. The letter E (or e) preceding the scale factor is pronounced as "times 10 to the power." Note that if a real number contains a decimal point, at least one digit must precede and follow the point.

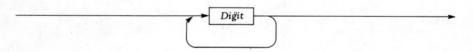

Figure 1.d   Syntax diagram for *UnsignedInteger*

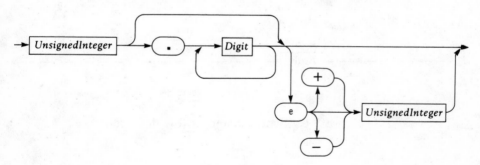

Figure 1.e   Syntax diagram for *UnsignedNumber*

Examples of unsigned numbers:
      3   03   6272844   0.6   5E–8   49.22E+08   1E10

Incorrectly written numbers:
      3,487,159   XII   .6   E10   5.E–16   five   3.487.159

1.E.   Character Strings

Sequences of characters enclosed by apostrophes (single quote marks) are called *strings*. To include an apostrophe in a string, write the apostrophe twice.

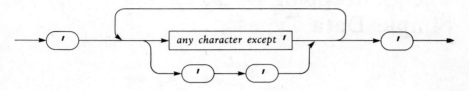

Figure 1.f   Syntax diagram for *CharacterString*

Examples of strings:
```
 'a'    ';'    '3'    'begin'    'don''t'
 '   This string has 33 characters.'
```

1.F.   Labels

Labels are unsigned integers used to mark a Pascal statement. Their apparent value must be in the range 0 to 9999.

Examples of labels:
```
 13    00100    9999
```

1.G.   Directives

Directives are names that substitute for procedure and function blocks. Directives have the same syntax as identifiers. (See Chapter 11.)

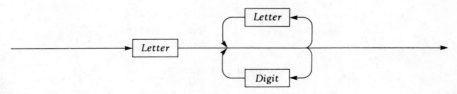

Figure 1.g   Syntax diagram for *Directive*

CHAPTER 2

The Concept of Data:
Simple Data Types

Data is the general term describing all that is operated on by a computer. At the hardware and machine-code levels, all data are represented as sequences of binary digits (bits). Higher-level languages allow one to use abstractions and to ignore the details of representation — largely by developing the concept of *data type*.

A data type defines the set of values a variable may assume and the operations which may be applied to it. Every variable occurring in a program must be associated with one and only one type. Although data types in Pascal can be quite sophisticated, each must be ultimately built from unstructured, simple types.

Pascal also provides facilities for creating collections of data types in the form of structured types and pointer types. These types are described in Chapters 6 through 10.

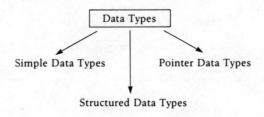

Figure 2.a   Type taxonomy of data types

The two kinds of simple types in Pascal are ordinal types and the real type. An ordinal type is either defined by you, and then called an enumerated or subrange type, or is denoted by one of the three predefined ordinal type identifiers — Boolean, Integer, or Char. The real type is denoted by the predefined type identifier Real.

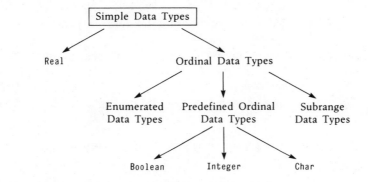

Figure 2.b   Type taxonomy of simple data types

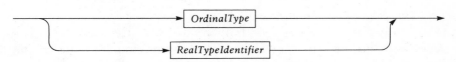

Figure 2.c   Syntax diagram for *SimpleType*

An enumerated type is characterized by the set of its distinct values, upon which a linear ordering is defined. The values are denoted by identifiers in the definition of the type. A subrange type specifies a minimum and maximum value of a previously declared ordinal type to create a new ordinal type. Enumerated and subrange types are described in Chapter 5.

2.A.   Ordinal Data Types

An ordinal data type describes a finite and ordered set of values. These values are mapped onto *ordinal numbers* 0, 1, 2, ..., except for the ordinal numbers of integers which are mapped onto themselves. Each ordinal type has a minimum and maximum value. Except for the minimum value, each value of an ordinal type has a *predecessor* value. Except for the maximum value, each value of an ordinal type has a *successor* value.

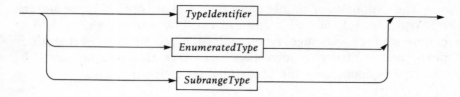

Figure 2.d   Syntax diagram for *OrdinalType*

The predeclared functions succ, pred, and ord accept arguments of any ordinal type:

succ(X)   the successor of X; yields the next ordinal value

pred(X)   the predecessor of X; yields the previous ordinal value

ord(X)   the ordinal-number function; yields the ordinal number of X.

The relational operators =, <>, <, <=, >=, and > are applicable to all ordinal types provided both operands are of the same type. The order is determined by the values of the ordinal numbers underlying the operands.

2.B.   The Type Boolean

A Boolean value is one of the logical truth values denoted by the predefined identifiers false and true.

The following logical operators yield a Boolean value when applied to Boolean operands: (Appendix B summarizes all operators.)

and   logical conjunction
or   logical disjunction
not   logical negation

Each of the relational operators (=, <>, <=, <, >, >=, in) yields a Boolean result. "<>" denotes inequality. Furthermore, the type Boolean is defined such that false < true. Hence, it is possible to define each of the 16 Boolean operations using the above logical and relational operators. For example, if P and Q are Boolean values, one can express

implication   as   P <= Q
equivalence   as   P = Q
exclusive or   as   P <> Q

Predeclared Boolean functions — i.e., predeclared functions which yield a Boolean result — are:

odd(I)   true if the integer I is odd, false otherwise.
eoln(F)   end of a line, explained in Chapter 9.
eof(F)   end of file, explained in Chapter 9.

(Appendix A summarizes all predeclared functions.)

2.C.   The Type Integer

A value of type Integer is an element of an implementation-defined subset of whole numbers.

The following arithmetic operators yield an integer value when applied to integer operands:

*   multiply

div   divide and truncate (i.e., value is not rounded)

mod   modulus:
    let Remainder = A − (A div B) * B;
    if Remainder < 0 then A mod B = Remainder + B
    otherwise A mod B = Remainder

+   add

−   subtract

There exists an implementation-defined, predefined constant identifier MaxInt specifying the largest integer value allowable for all integer operations. If A and B are integer expressions, the operation:

A op B

is guaranteed to be correctly implemented when:

abs(A op B)   <=   MaxInt,
abs(A)   <=   MaxInt, and
abs(B)   <=   MaxInt

Four important predeclared functions yielding integer results are:

abs(I)   the absolute value of the integer value I.

sqr(I)   the integer value I squared, assuming I <= MaxInt div
I.

trunc(R)   R is a real value: the result is its whole part. (The
fractional part is discarded. Hence trunc(3.7) = 3 and
trunc(-3.7) = -3).

round(R)   R is a real value: the result is the rounded integer.
round(R) for R >= 0 means trunc(R + 0.5) and for R < 0
means trunc(R - 0.5).

If I is an integer value, then

succ(I)   yields the "next" integer (I + 1), and
pred(I)   yields the preceding integer (I - 1).

2.D.   The Type Char

A value of type Char is an element of a finite and ordered set of
characters. Every computer system defines such a set for the purpose
of communication. These characters are then available on the input
and output equipment. Unfortunately, there does not exist one standard character set; therefore, the elements and their ordering is
strictly implementation-defined. (See Appendix G.)

A character enclosed in apostrophes (single quotes) denotes a
value of this type.

Examples:
'*'   'G'   '3'   ''''   'X'

(To represent an apostrophe, write it twice.) However, it is possible
that some character values have no constant representation.

The following minimal assumptions hold for the type Char, independent of the underlying implementation:

1. The decimal digits '0' through '9' are numerically ordered
   and consecutive (e.g., succ('5') = '6').

2. Upper-case letters 'A' through 'Z' may exist; if so, they are
   alphabetically ordered, but not necessarily consecutive (e.g.,
   'A' < 'B').

3. Lower-case letters 'a' through 'z' may exist; if so, they are alphabetically ordered, but not necessarily consecutive (e.g., 'a' < 'b').

The two predeclared functions ord and chr allow the mapping of the given character set onto the ordinal numbers of the character set — and vice versa; ord and chr are called *transfer functions*.

ord(C)	is the ordinal number of the character C in the underlying ordered character set.
chr(I)	is the character value with the ordinal number I.

You can see immediately that ord and chr are inverse functions, i.e.,

chr(ord(C)) = C   and   ord(chr(I)) = I

Furthermore, the ordering of a given character set is defined by

C1 < C2   iff   ord(C1) < ord(C2)

This definition can be extended to each of the relational operators: =, <>, <, <=, >=, >. If R denotes one of these operators, then

C1 R C2   iff   ord(C1) R ord(C2)

When the argument of the predeclared functions pred and succ is of type Char, the functions can be defined as:

pred(C) = chr(ord(C)−1)
succ(C) = chr(ord(C)+1)

Note: The predecessor (successor) of a character is dependent upon the underlying character set. The two properties hold only if the predecessor or successor exists.

2.E.   The Type Real

A value of type Real is an element of the implementation-defined subset of real numbers.

All operations on values of type Real are approximations, the accuracy of which is defined by the implementation (machine) that you are using. Real is the only simple type that is not an ordinal type. Real values have no ordinal numbers, and for any real value there is no successor or predecessor value.

As long as at least one of the operands is of type Real (the other possibly being of type Integer) the following operators yield a real value:

*   multiply

/   divide (both operands may be integers, but the result is always real)

+   add

−   subtract

These predeclared functions accept a real argument and yield a real result:

abs(R)   absolute value of R

sqr(R)   R squared, if the resulting value doesn't exceed the range of real numbers

These predeclared functions accept a real or integer argument and yield a real result:

sin(X)   sine of X, X in radians
cos(X)   cosine of X, X in radians
arctan(X) arc tangant in radians of X
ln(X)   natural logarithm (to the base e) of X, X > 0
exp(X)   exponential function (e raised to the X)
sqrt(X)   square root of X, X >= 0.

Warning: Although real is included as a simple type, it cannot always be used in the same context as the other simple types (i.e., ordinal types). In particular, the functions pred and succ cannot take real arguments; and values of type Real cannot be used when indexing arrays, nor in controlling for statements, nor for defining the base type of a set. Furthermore reals cannot be used in a subrange type nor to index a case statement.

CHAPTER 3

The Program Heading and
The Declaration Part

Every program consists of a heading and a block. The block contains a declaration part, in which all objects local to the program are defined, and a statement part, which specifies the actions to be executed upon these objects.

Figure 3.a   Syntax diagram for *Program*

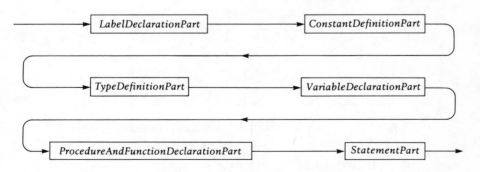

Figure 3.b   Syntax diagram for *Block*

Figure 3.c   Syntax diagram for *StatementPart*

3.A.   Program Heading

The heading gives the program a name (not otherwise significant inside the program) and lists its parameters that denote entities that exist outside the program and through which the program communicates with the environment. The entities (usually files — see Chapter 9) are called *external*. Each parameter must be declared in the block constituting the program, just as an ordinary local variable (see Section E.).

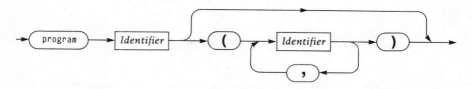

Figure 3.d   Syntax diagram for *ProgramHeading*

3.B.   Label Declaration Part

Any statement in a program may be marked by prefixing the statement with a label followed by a colon (making possible a reference by a goto statement). However, the label must be declared in the *label declaration part* before its use. The symbol label heads this part, which has the general form:

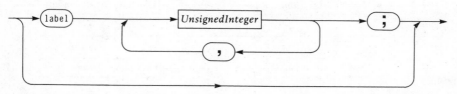

Figure 3.e   Syntax diagram for *LabelDeclarationPart*

A label is defined to be an unsigned integer, with a value in the range 0 to 9999.

Example:
```
label   13, 00100, 99;
```

3.C.   Constant Definition Part

A *constant definition* introduces an identifier as a synonym for a constant. The symbol const heads the constant definition part, which has the general form:

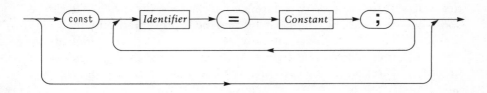

Figure 3.f   Syntax diagram for *ConstantDefinitionPart*

where a constant is either a number, a constant identifier (possibly signed), a character, or a string.

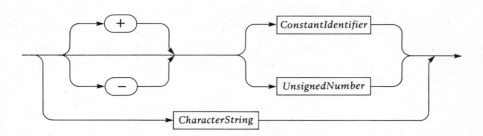

Figure 3.g   Syntax diagram for *Constant*

The use of constant identifiers generally makes a program more readable and acts as a convenient documentation aid. It also allows you to group machine- or example-dependent quantities at the beginning of the program where they can be easily noted and changed or both. This improves the portability and modularity of the program.

Example:
```
const
    Avogadro   = 6.023E23;
    PageLength = 60;
    Border     = '# * ';
    MyMove     = True;
```

3.D.   Type Definition Part

A data type in Pascal may be either directly described in a variable declaration (see below) or referenced by a *type identifier.* There are some places in Pascal where a type may be represented only by a type identifier. Pascal provides not only several standard type identifiers, but also a mechanism, the *type definition,* for introducing a new type identifier to represent a type. The symbol type heads a program part containing type definitions. The general form is:

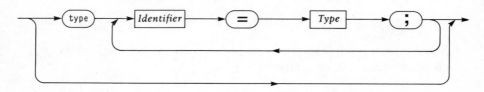

Figure 3.h   Syntax diagram for *TypeDefinitionPart*

Note that *Type* represents a simple type, structured type, or pointer-type, and consists of either a type-identifier denoting an existing type or else a new type description.

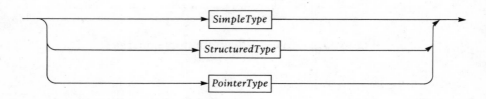

Figure 3.i   Syntax diagram for *Type*

Examples of type definitions are found throughout the remainder of the User Manual.

3.E.   Variable Declaration Part

Every variable identifier occurring in a program must be introduced in a *variable declaration*. This declaration must textually precede any use of the variable, unless the variable is a program parameter.

A variable declaration introduces a variable identifier and its associated data type by simply listing the identifier followed by the type. The symbol var heads the variable declaration part. The general form is:

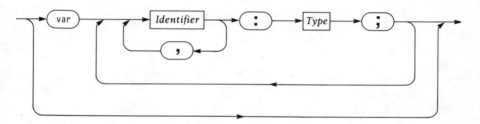

Figure 3.j   Syntax diagram for *VariableDeclarationPart*

Example:
```
var
    Root1, Root2, Root3: Real:
    Count, I: Integer;
    Found: Boolean;
    Filler: Char;
```

Any identifier (denoting an external entity — usually a file) listed in the program heading parameter list except Input or Output must be declared in the program's variable declaration part. Input or Output, if listed, are automatically declared to be textfiles (see Chapter 9).

```
program TemperatureConversion(Output);

    { Program 3.1 - Example program illustrating constant and type
                    definition parts and variable declaration part. }

    const
        Bias = 32;  Factor = 1.8;  Low = -20;  High = 39;
        Separator = '   ---';  Blanks = '          ';

    type
        CelciusRange = Low..High { a subrange type-see Chapter 5 };
```

```
    var
        Degree: CelciusRange;

begin
    for Degree := Low to High do
        begin
            Write(Output, Degree, ' C');
            Write(Output, Separator, Round(Degree * Factor + Bias), ' F');
            if odd(Degree) then Writeln(Output)
            else Write(Output, Blanks)
        end;
    Writeln(Output)
end .
```

Produces as results:

-20 C	---	-4 F		-19 C	---	-2 F
-18 C	---	0 F		-17 C	---	1 F
-16 C	---	3 F		-15 C	---	5 F
-14 C	---	7 F		-13 C	---	9 F
-12 C	---	10 F		-11 C	---	12 F
-10 C	---	14 F		-9 C	---	16 F
-8 C	---	18 F		-7 C	---	19 F
-6 C	---	21 F		-5 C	---	23 F
-4 C	---	25 F		-3 C	---	27 F
-2 C	---	28 F		-1 C	---	30 F
0 C	---	32 F		1 C	---	34 F
2 C	---	36 F		3 C	---	37 F
4 C	---	39 F		5 C	---	41 F
6 C	---	43 F		7 C	---	45 F
8 C	---	46 F		9 C	---	48 F
10 C	---	50 F		11 C	---	52 F
12 C	---	54 F		13 C	---	55 F
14 C	---	57 F		15 C	---	59 F
16 C	---	61 F		17 C	---	63 F
18 C	---	64 F		19 C	---	66 F
20 C	---	68 F		21 C	---	70 F
22 C	---	72 F		23 C	---	73 F
24 C	---	75 F		25 C	---	77 F
26 C	---	79 F		27 C	---	81 F
28 C	---	82 F		29 C	---	84 F
30 C	---	86 F		31 C	---	88 F
32 C	---	90 F		33 C	---	91 F
34 C	---	93 F		35 C	---	95 F
36 C	---	97 F		37 C	---	99 F
38 C	---	100 F		39 C	---	102 F

3.F.   Procedure and Function Declaration Part

Every procedure or function identifier must be declared before its use. Procedure and function declarations take the same form as a program —a heading followed by a block — see Chapter 11 for details and examples. Procedures are subprograms that are activated by procedure statements. Functions are subprograms that yield a result value, and are used as constituents of expressions.

3.G.   Scope of Identifiers and Labels

The declaration or definition of an identifier (constant, type, variable, procedure, or function identifier) or label holds for the entire block containing the definition or declaration, except for any *nested* (subordinate) block in which the identifier or label is redeclared or redefined. The region over which the declaration or definition of an identifier or label applies is called the scope of that identifier or label.

An identifier or label declared or defined in the program block is said to be *global*. An identifier or label is said to be *local* to the block where it is declared or defined. An identifier or label is *non-local* to a block if it is declared or defined in an enclosing block. See Section 0.D for examples.

You cannot declare a single identifier more than once within the same level and scope. Hence the following is incorrect:

```
var  X: Integer;
     X: Char;
```

CHAPTER 4

The Concept of Action

Essential to a computer program is action. That is, a program must do something with its data — even if that action is the choice of doing nothing! *Statements* describe these actions. Statements are either *simple* (e.g., the assignment statement) or *structured*. See the syntax diagram for *Statement* (Figure 4.a).

4.A.   The Assignment Statement and Expressions

The most fundamental of statements is the *assignment statement*. It specifies that a newly computed value be assigned to a variable. The value is specified by an expression. Assignment statements have the form shown in Figure 4.b. The := symbol denotes *assignment* and is not to be confused with the relational operator =. The statement "A := 5" is pronounced "the current value of A is replaced with the value 5," or simply, "A becomes 5."

A *variable* (see Figure 4.c) may be an *entire variable* representing all the data storage for a simple, structured, or pointer type. In the case of structured types (see Chapters 6 through 9), a variable may be a *component variable* or a *buffer variable* representing one component of the data storage. For pointer types, a variable may be an *identified variable* representing data storage indirectly referenced by a pointer.

An *expression* consists of operators and operands. An operand may be a constant, variable, array-parameter bound (discussed in

Chapter 11), or function designator. (A function designator specifies activation of a function. Predeclared functions are listed in Appendix A; user-declared functions are explained in Chapter 11.)

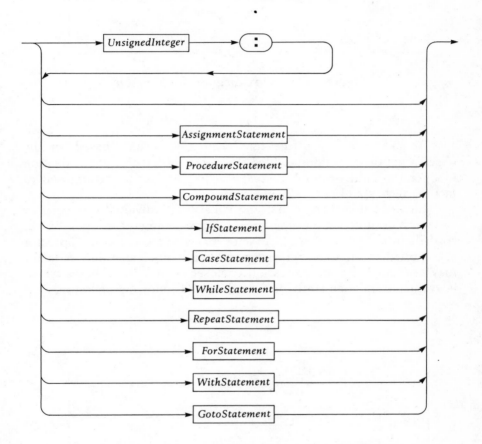

Figure 4.a   Syntax diagram for *Statement*

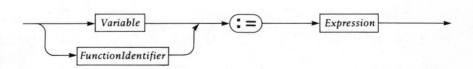

Figure 4.b   Syntax diagram for *AssignmentStatement*

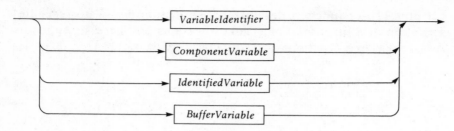

Figure 4.c   Syntax diagram for *Variable*

An *expression* is a rule for calculating a value based on the observation of conventional rules of algebra for left-to-right evaluation of operators and *operator precedence*. Expressions are composed of factors, terms, and simple expressions.

Factors are evaluated first and consist of individual constants or variables or function designators or array-parameter bounds or set constructors (see Chapter 8). A factor may also consist of the operator not applied to another factor representing a Boolean value. A factor may also comprise an expression enclosed within parentheses which is evaluated independently of preceding and following operators.

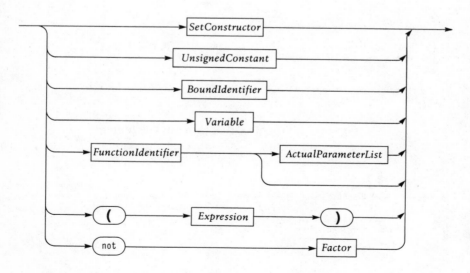

Figure 4.d   Syntax diagram for *Factor*

Terms are evaluated next and consist of a sequence of factors, separated by multiplying operators (*, /, div, mod, and) or alternatively, simply a factor by itself.

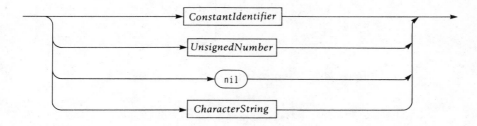

Figure 4.e   Syntax diagram for *UnsignedConstant*

Simple expressions are evaluated after terms and consist of a sequence of terms, separated by adding operators (+, −, or) or alternatively, simply a term by itself. An optional sign-inversion operator (+, −) may prefix the first term of a simple expression.

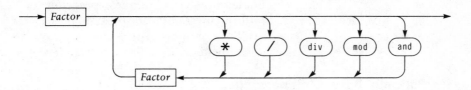

Figure 4.f   Syntax diagram for *Term*

Finally expressions are evaluated. These comprise a simple expression, a relational operator (=, <>, <=, >=, >, in) and another simple expression, or simply a simple expression itself.

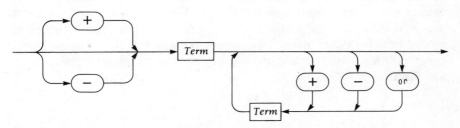

Figure 4.g   Syntax diagram for *SimpleExpression*

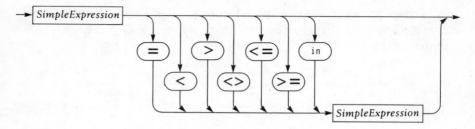

Figure 4.h   Syntax diagram for *Expression*

Examples:

```
2 * 3-4 * 5          =  (2*3) - (4*5)  =  -14
15 div 4 * 4         =  (15 div 4)*4   =  12
80/5/3               =  (80/5)/3       =  5.333
4/2 *3               =  (4/2)*3        =  6.000
sqrt(sqr(3)+11*5)                      =  8.000
```

We recommend that you refer to the table below whenever in doubt of the exact rules of operator precedence.

Operator	Classification
not	Boolean negation (highest precedence)
*, /, div, mod, and	Multiplying operators (next highest)
+, -, or	Adding operators (third highest)
=, <>, <, <=, >=, >, in	Relational operators (lowest precedence).

See Appendix B for a full description of operators.

Boolean expressions have the property that their value may be known before the entire expression has been evaluated. Assume for example, that X = 0. Then the value of the expression

```
(X > 0) and (X < 10)
```

is already known to be false after computation of the first factor and the second need not be evaluated. Whether or not the second factor is evaluated is implementation-dependent. This means that you must assure that the second factor is well-defined, independent of the value of the first factor. Hence, if we assume that the array A has an index ranging from 1 to 10, then the following example is in error! (Arrays are discussed in Chapter 6.)

```
X := 0;
repeat X := X + 1 until (X > 10) or (A[X] = 0)
```

(Note that if no A[I] = 0, the program will refer to an element A[11].)

Except for file variables (see Chapter 9), assignment is possible to variables of any type. The variable (or the function) and the expression must be *assignment compatible*. All the cases for assignment-compatibility are listed below:

1. The variable and the expression are the same type except if that type is a file type (see Chapter 9) or contains a file type as a component in another structured type.

2. The variable is real type and the expression is integer type.

3. The variable and the expression are the same or subranges (see Chapter 5) of the same ordinal type, and the value of the expression lies within the closed interval specified by the type of the variable.

4. The variable and the expression are the same set type (see Chapter 8) or are set types with base types which are the same or subranges of the same ordinal type. Either both types or neither type must be packed. The value of the expression must be a value of the type of the variable.

5. The variable and the expression are string types (see Section 6.B) with the same number of elements.

Examples of assignments:
```
Root1 := Pi*X/Y
Root2 := -Root1
Root3 := (Root1 + Root2)*(1.0 + Y)
Danger := Temp > VaporPoint
Count  := Count + 1
Degree := Degree + 10
SqrPr  := sqr(pr)
Y      := sin(X) + cos(Y)
```

4.B. The Procedure Statement

Another kind of simple statement is the *procedure statement,* which activates the named procedure which is a subprogram specifying another set of actions to be performed on data. So far in this tutorial we have used the procedures Read, Readln, Write, and Writeln to perform input and output. Procedure statements are discussed fully in Chapter 11.

4.C.   The Compound Statement and the Empty Statement

The *compound statement* specifies that its component statements be executed in the same sequence as they are written. The symbols begin and end act as statement brackets. Note that the statement part or "body" of a program has the form of a compound statement.

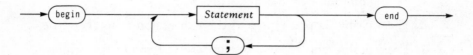

Figure 4.i   Syntax diagram for *CompoundStatement*

```
program BeginEndExample(Output);

   { Program 4.1 - Illustrate the compound statement. }

   var
      Sum: Integer;

begin
   Sum := 3 + 5;
   Writeln(Output, Sum, -Sum)
end .
```

Produces as results:

```
        8        -8
```

Pascal uses the semicolon to *separate* statements, not to terminate statements; i.e., the semicolon is NOT part of the statement. The explicit rules regarding semicolons are reflected in the syntax of Appendix D. If one had written a semicolon after the second statement in Program 4.1, then an *empty statement* (implying no action) would have been assumed between the semicolon and the symbol end. This does no harm, for an empty statement is allowable at this point. Misplaced semicolons can, however, cause troubles — note the example for if statements in Section 4.E.

4.D.   Repetitive Statements

Repetitive statements specify that certain statements be repeatedly executed. If the number of repetitions is known beforehand (before the repetitions are begun), the for statement is usually the appropriate construct you can use to express the situation; otherwise use the repeat or while statement.

4.D.1   The while statement

The while statement has the form:

Figure 4.j   Syntax diagram for *WhileStatement*

The statement following the symbol do is executed zero or more times. The expression controlling the repetition must be of type Boolean. Before the statement is executed the expression is evaluated; the statement is executed if the expression is true, otherwise the while statement terminates. Because the expression is evaluated for each iteration, you must be careful to keep the expression as simple as possible.

Program 4.3 raises a real value X to the power Y, where Y is a non-negative integer. A simpler, and evidently correct, version is obtained by omitting the inner while statement: the variable Result is then obtained through Y multiplications by X. Note the loop invariant: Result*power(Base,Exponent) = power(X,Y). The inner while statement leaves Result and power(Base,Exponent) invariant, and obviously improves the efficiency of the algorithm.

4.D.2   The repeat statement

The repeat statement has the form:

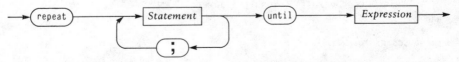

Figure 4.k   Syntax diagram for *RepeatStatement*

```
program WhileExample(Input,Output);

    { Program 4.2 - Compute the Nth partial sum of the harmonic
                    series H(N) = 1 + 1/2 + 1/3 + ... + 1/N
                    using a while statement for iteration. }

    var
        N: Integer;
        H: Real;
begin
    Read(Input,N);   Write(Output,N);
    H := 0;
    while N > 0 do
        begin
            H := H + 1/N;   N := N - 1
        end;
    Writeln(Output,H)
end .
```

Produces as results:

```
    10 2.928968E+00
```

```
program Exponentiation(Input, Output);

    { Program 4.3 - Compute power(X,Y) using natural exponent;
                where power(X,Y) means "X raised to the power Y". }

    var
        Exponent, Y: Integer;
        Base, Result, X: Real;
begin  Read(Input,X,Y);   Writeln(Output,X,Y);
    Result := 1;   Base := X;   Exponent := Y;
    while Exponent > 0 do
        begin
            { Result*power(Base,Exponent) = power(X,Y),Exponent > 0 }
            while not Odd(Exponent) do
                begin  Exponent := Exponent div 2;   Base := Sqr(Base)
                end;
            Exponent := Exponent - 1;   Result := Result * Base
        end;
    Writeln(Output,Result) { Result = power(X,Y) }
end .
```

Produces as results:

```
 2.000000E+00          7
 1.280000E+02
```

The sequence of statements between the symbols repeat and until is executed at least once. After each execution of the sequence of statements the Boolean expression is evaluated. Repeated execution is continued until the expression becomes true. Because the expression is evaluated for every iteration, you must be careful to keep it as simple as possible.

```
program RepeatExample(Input,Output);

    { Program 4.4 - Compute the Nth partial sum of the harmonic
                    series  H(N) = 1 + 1/2 + 1/3 + ... + 1/N
                    using a repeat statement for iteration. }
    var
        N: Integer;
        H: Real;
begin
    Read(Input,N);  Write(Output,N);
    H := 0;
    repeat
        H := H + 1/N;  N := N - 1
    until N = 0;
    Writeln(Output,H)
end .
```

Produces as results:

        10 2.928968E+00

The above program performs correctly for N > 0. Consider what happens if N <= 0. The while-version of the same program is correct for all N, including N = 0.

Note that it is a sequence of statements that the repeat statement executes; a bracketing pair begin...end would be redundant (but not incorrect).

4.D.3   The for statement

The for statement indicates that a statement be repeatedly executed while a progression of values is assigned to the *control variable* of the for statement. It has the general form:

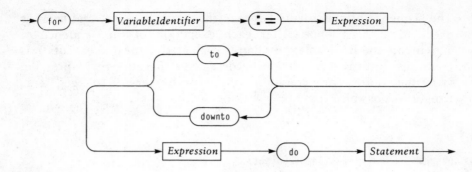

Figure 4.1   Syntax diagram for *ForStatement*

```
program ForExample(Input,Output);

    { Program 4.5 - Compute the Nth partial sum of the harmonic
                    series  H(N) = 1 + 1/2 + 1/3 + ... + 1/N
                    using a for statement for iteration. }

    var
       I, N: Integer;
       H: Real;
begin
    Read(Input,N);  Write(Output,N);
    H := 0;
    for I := N downto 1 do
       H := H + 1/I;
    Writeln(Output,H)
end .
```

Produces as results:

```
10 2.928968E+00
```

The control variable, which appears following the symbol for must be
of an ordinal type and declared in the same block that the for
statement appears. The initial value and the final value must be of an
ordinal type compatible with the control variable. The control variable
must not be altered by the component statement. This prohibits its
appearing as a variable on the left-hand side of an assignment, in a

Read or Readln procedure or as the control variable of another for statement, either directly within the for statement or within a procedure or function declared within the same block. The initial and final values are evaluated only once. If in the case of to (downto) the initial value is greater (less) than the final value, the component statement is not executed. If the component statement is executed, it is an error if either the initial value or final value cannot be assigned to the control variable. The control variable is left undefined upon normal exit from the for statement.

```
program Cosine(Input,Output);

    { Program 4.6 - Compute the cosine using the expansion:
                    cos(X) = 1 - sqr(X)/(2*1)
                             + sqr(X)*sqr(X)/(4*3*2*1) - ... }

    const
        Epsilon = 1e-7;

    var
            Angle: Real    { radians };
         ASquared: Real    { Angle squared };
           Series: Real    { cosine series };
             Term: Real    { next term in series };
          I, N: Integer    { number of cosines to compute };
          Power: Integer   { power of next term };

begin
    Readln(Input,N);
    for I := 1 to N do
        begin
            Readln(Input,Angle);
            Term := 1;  Power := 0;  Series := 1;
            ASquared := Sqr(Angle);
            while Abs(Term) > Epsilon * Abs(Series) do
                begin
                    Power := Power + 2;
                    Term := -Term * Asquared / (Power * (Power - 1));
                    Series := Series + Term
                end;
            Writeln(Output, Angle, Series, Power div 2
                { = terms to convergence })
        end
end .
```

Produces as results:

```
1.534622E-01 9.882478E-01        3
3.333333E-01 9.449569E-01        4
5.000000E-01 8.775826E-01        5
1.000000E+00 5.403023E-01        6
3.141593E+00-1.000000E+00       10
```

The following program plots a real-valued function f(X) by letting the X-axis run vertically and then writing an asterisk in positions corresponding to the coordinates. The position of the asterisk is obtained by computing Y = f(X), multiplying by a scale factor, rounding the product to the next integer, and then adding a constant and letting the asterisk be preceded by that many blank spaces.

```pascal
program Graph1(Output);

    { Program 4.7 - Generate graphic representation of the
                    function: f(X) = exp(-X) * sin(2*Pi*X). }

    const
        XLines = 16 { line spacings per 1 abscissa unit };
        Scale = 32  { character widths per 1 ordinate unit };
        ZeroY = 34  { character position of X axis };
        XLimit = 32 { length of graph in lines };

    var
        Delta: Real { increment along abscissa };
        TwoPi: Real { 2 * Pi = 8 * ArcTan(1.0) };
        X, Y : Real;
        Point: Integer;
        YPosition: Integer;

begin { initialize constants: }
    Delta := 1 / Xlines;
    TwoPi := 8 * ArcTan(1.0);
```

```
for Point := 0 to XLimit do
   begin
      X := Delta * Point;   Y := Exp(-X) * Sin(TwoPi * X);
      YPosition := Round(Scale * Y) + ZeroY;
      repeat
         Write(Output, ' ');   YPosition := YPosition - 1
      until YPosition = 0;
      Writeln(Output, '*')
   end
end .
```

Produces as results:

```
                              *
                                   *
                                     *
                                       *
                                       *
                                     *
                                  *
                               *
                           *
                        *
                    *
                    *
                     *
                       *
                          *
                             *
                               *
                                *
                                 *
                                *
                               *
                             *
                           *
                         *
                       *
                      *
                     *
                    *
                   *
                   *
                    *
```

As a final example consider the following program.

```pascal
program SummingTerms(Output);

  { Program 4.8 - Compute the series
                    1 - 1/2 + 1/3 - ... + 1/9999 - 1/10000
                  four ways:
                  1) left to right in succession,
                  2) left to right, all pos and neg terms then
                        subtract,
                  3) right to left in succession, and
                  4) right to left, all pos and neg terms then
                        subtract. }

  var
      SeriesLR,            { series sum, left to right in succession }
      SumLRPosTerms,       { sum of positive terms, left to right }
      SumLRNegTerms,       { sum of negative terms, left to right }
      SeriesRL,            { series sum, right to left in succession }
      SumRLPosTerms,       { sum of positive terms, right to left }
      SumRLNegTerms,       { sum of negative terms, right to left }
      PosTermLR,           { next positive term, left to right }
      NegTermLR,           { next negative term, left to right }
      PosTermRL,           { next positive term, right to left }
      NegTermRL: Real      { next negative term, right to left };
      PairsOfTerms: Integer { count of pairs of terms };

begin
    SeriesLR := 0;  SumLRPosTerms := 0;  SumLRNegTerms := 0;
    SeriesRL := 0;  SumRLPosTerms := 0;  SumRLNegTerms := 0;
    for PairsOfTerms := 1 to 5000 do
      begin
          PosTermLR := 1 / (2 * PairsOfTerms - 1);
          NegTermLR := 1 / (2 * PairsOfTerms);
          PosTermRL := 1 / (10001 - 2 * PairsOfTerms);
          NegTermRL := 1 / (10002 - 2 * PairsOfTerms);
          SeriesLR := SeriesLR + PosTermLR - NegTermLR;
          SumLRPosTerms := SumLRPosTerms + PosTermLR;
          SumLRNegTerms := SumLRNegTerms + NegTermLR;
          SeriesRL := SeriesRL + PosTermRL - NegTermRL;
          SumRLPosTerms := SumRLPosTerms + PosTermRL;
          SumRLNegTerms := SumRLNegTerms + NegTermRL;
      end;
```

```
Writeln(Output, SeriesLR);
Writeln(Output, SumLRPosTerms - SumLRNegTerms);
Writeln(Output, SeriesRL);
Writeln(Output, SumRLPosTerms - SumRLNegTerms)
```

end .

Produces as results:

```
6.930919E-01
6.931014E-01
6.930970E-01
6.930971E-01
```

Why do the four "identical" sums differ?

4.E.   Conditional Statements

A *conditional statement* selects a single statement of its component statements for execution. Pascal offers two kinds of conditional statements, the if and case statements.

4.E.1   The if statement

The *if statement* specifies that a statement be executed only if a certain condition (Boolean expression) is true. If it is false, then either no statement or the statement following the symbol else is executed.
     The form of an if statement is:

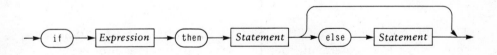

Figure 4.m   Syntax diagram for *IfStatement*

     The expression between the symbols if and then must be of type Boolean. Note that the first form may be regarded as an abbreviation of the second when the alternative statement is the empty statement. Caution: there is never a semicolon before an else! Hence, the text:

```
if P then begin S1; S2; S3 end; else S4
```

is incorrect. More deceptive is the text:

```
if P then; begin S1; S2; S3 end
```

Here, the statement controlled by the if is the empty statement between the then and the semicolon; hence, the compound statement following the if statement will always be executed.

The syntactic ambiguity arising from the construct:

```
if expression1 then if expression2 then statement1
    else statement2
```

is resolved by interpreting the construct as equivalent to

```
if expression1 then
    begin if expression2 then statement1
        else statement2
    end
```

You are further cautioned that a carelessly formulated if statement can be very costly. Take the example where there are n *mutually exclusive* conditions, C1...Cn, each instigating a distinct action, Si. Let P(Ci) be the probability of Ci being true, and say that P(Ci) >= P(Cj) for i < j. Then the most efficient sequence of if clauses is:

```
if C1 then S1
    else if C2 then S2
        else  ...
            else if C(n-1) then S(n-1) else Sn
```

The fulfillment of a condition and the execution of its statement completes the if statement, thereby bypassing the remaining tests.

If Found is a variable of type Boolean, another frequent abuse of the if statement can be illustrated by:

```
if Key = ValueSought then Found := true else Found := false
```

A much simpler statement is:

```
Found := Key = ValueSought
```

```
program ArabicToRoman(Output);

   { Program 4.9 - Write a table of powers of 2 in
                    Arabic numbers and Roman numerals. }

   var
      Rem { remainder },
      Number: Integer;
begin
   Number := 1;
   repeat
      Write(Output, Number, ' ');
      Rem := Number;
      while Rem >= 1000 do
         begin  Write(Output, 'M');   Rem := Rem - 1000  end;
      if Rem >= 900 then
         begin  Write(Output, 'CM');   Rem := Rem - 900  end
      else
         if Rem >= 500 then
            begin  Write(Output, 'D');   Rem := Rem - 500  end
         else
            if Rem >= 400 then
               begin  Write(Output, 'CD');   Rem := Rem - 400  end;
      while Rem >= 100 do
         begin  Write(Output, 'C');   Rem := Rem - 100  end;
      if Rem >= 90 then
         begin  Write(Output, 'XC');   Rem := Rem - 90  end
      else
         if Rem >= 50 then
            begin  Write(Output, 'L');   Rem := Rem - 50  end
         else
            if Rem >= 40 then
               begin  Write(Output, 'XL');   Rem := Rem - 40  end;
      while Rem >= 10 do
         begin  Write(Output, 'X');   Rem := Rem - 10  end;
      if Rem = 9 then
         begin  Write(Output, 'IX');   Rem := Rem - 9  end
      else
         if Rem >= 5 then
            begin  Write(Output, 'V');   Rem := Rem - 5  end
         else
            if Rem = 4 then
               begin  Write(Output, 'IV');   Rem := Rem - 4  end;
      while Rem >= 1 do
         begin  Write(Output, 'I');   Rem := Rem - 1;  end;
      Writeln(Output);
      Number := Number * 2
   until Number > 5000
end .
```

Produces as results:

```
   1 I
   2 II
   4 IV
   8 VIII
  16 XVI
  32 XXXII
  64 LXIV
 128 CXXVIII
 256 CCLVI
 512 DXII
1024 MXXIV
2048 MMXLVIII
4096 MMMMXCVI
```

Notice again that each "branch" of an if statement consists of only one statement. Therefore, when more than one action is intended, a compound statement is necessary.

4.E.2   The case statement

The case statement consists of an expression (the selector) and a list of statements, each being associated with one or more constant values of the type of the selector. The selector type must be an ordinal type. Each constant value must be associated with at most one of the statements. The case statement selects for execution the statement that is associated with the current value of the selector; if no such constant is listed, it is an error. Upon completion of the selected statement, control goes to the end of the case statement. The form is:

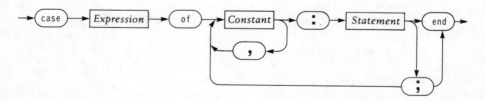

Figure 4.n   Syntax diagram for *CaseStatement*

Examples: (Assume `var i: Integer; ch: Char;`)

```
case i of
   0: x := 0;
   1: x := sin(x);
   2: x := cos(x);
   3: x := exp(x);
   4: x := ln(x)
end

case ch of
   'a', 'A', 'e', 'E', 'i',
   'I', 'o', 'O', 'u', 'U':
      vowel := vowel + 1;
   '+', '-', '*', '/', '=', '>', '<',
   '.', ',', '"', '?', '!', ':', ';', '''':
      punc := punc + 1
end
```

Notes: Case constants are NOT labels (see Sections 3.B and 4.G) and cannot be referenced by a goto statement; their ordering is arbitrary.

Although the efficiency of the case statement depends on the implementation, the general rule is to use it when one has several mutually exclusive statements with similar probability of selection.

4.F.   The With Statement

A *with statement* is used in conjunction with variables having a record type (a structured type). It is discussed in Section 7.C.

4.G.   The Goto Statement

A *goto statement* is a simple statement indicating that further processing should continue at another part of the program text, namely at the place of the label.

Figure 4.0   Syntax diagram for *GotoStatement*

Each label

1. must appear in the label declaration *prior* to its occurrence in the block.

2. must prefix *one and only* one statement appearing in the statement part of the block.

3. has a scope over the *entire text* of that block excepting any nested blocks that redeclare the label.

At least one of the following three conditions must hold for labels and the goto statements which refer to them:

1. The label prefixes a statement which contains the goto statement.

2. The label prefixes a statement in a statement sequence (within a compound statement or repeat statement) and any statement in the statement sequence contains the goto statement.

3. The label prefixes a statement in the statement sequence forming the statement part of a block that contains a procedure or function declaration that contains the goto statement.

Example: (program fragment):

```
label 1; { block A }
    ...
    procedure B; { block B }
        label 3, 5;
    begin
        goto 3;
    3: Writeln('Hello');
    5: if P then begin S; goto 5 end; { while P do S }
        goto 1;
        { this causes early termination of the activation of B }
        Writeln('Goodbye')
    end; { block B }

begin
    B;
1: Writeln(' Edsger')
    { a "goto 3" is not allowed in block A }
end { block A }
```

Jumps from outside of a structured statement into that statement are not allowed. Hence, the following examples are incorrect.

Incorrect examples:

a) ```
for I := 1 to 10 do
    begin S1;
    3: S2
    end;
goto 3
```

b) ```
if B then goto 3;
    ...
if B1 then 3: S
```

c) ```
procedure P:
    procedure Q;
    begin ...
        3: S
    end;
begin ...
    goto 3
end.
```

A goto statement should be reserved for unusual or uncommon situations where the natural structure of an algorithm has to be broken. A good rule is to avoid the use of jumps to express regular iterations and conditional execution of statements, for such jumps destroy the reflection of the structure of computation in the textual (static) structures of the program. Moreover, the lack of correspondence between textual and computational (static and dynamic) structure is extremely detrimental to the clarity of the program and makes the task of verification much more difficult. The presence of goto's in a Pascal program is often an indication that the programmer has not yet learned "to think" in Pascal (as the goto is a necessary construct in some other programming languages).
```

CHAPTER 5

Enumerated and Subrange Types

We have seen the predefined, simple type identifiers Boolean, Char, Integer and Real. By using these type identifiers you can refer to the existing types that they represent. We now show how new ordinal types can be created by two mechanisms: the enumerated type and the subrange type. The enumerated type creates a new type that is unrelated to any other type, while the subrange type creates a new type that has a subset of the values of another existing ordinal type.

5.A. Enumerated Types

An enumerated type definition specifies an ordered set of values by enumerating the constant identifiers which denote the values.

The ordinal number of the first constant listed is 0; the second one is 1, etc.

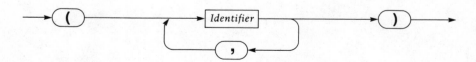

Figure 5.a   Syntax diagram for *EnumeratedType*

Example:
```
type Color = (White, Red, Blue, Yellow, Purple, Green,
              Orange, Black);
     Sex = (Male, Female);
     Day = (Mon, Tue, Wed, Thu, Fri, Sat, Sun);
     Operators = (Plus, Minus, Times, Divide);
     Continent = (Africa, Antarctica, Asia, Australia, Europe,
              NorthAmerica, SouthAmerica)
```

Incorrect example:
```
type Workday = (Mon, Tues, Wed, Thur, Fri, Sat);
     Free = (Sat, Sun);
```

because the type of Sat is ambiguous.

You are already acquainted with the predefined type Boolean defined as:

```
type Boolean = (false, true);
```

This automatically defines the constant identifiers false and true and specifies that false < true.

The relational operators =, <>, <, <=, >=, and >, are applicable to all enumerated types provided both operands are of the same type. The order is determined by the sequence in which the constants are listed.

Predeclared functions with arguments of ordinal types are:

```
succ(X)    e.g.  succ(Blue) = Yellow   the successor of X
pred(X)          pred(Blue) = Red      the predecessor of X
ord(X)           ord(Blue) = 2         the ordinal number of X
```

Assuming that C and C1 are of type Color (above), B is of type Boolean, and S1...Sn are arbitrary statements, then the following are meaningful statements:

```
for C := Black downto Red do S1
while (C1 <> C) and B do S1
if C > White then C := pred(C)
case C of
   Red, Blue, Yellow: S1;
   Purple: S2;
   Green, Orange: S3;
   White, Black: S4
end .
```

Program 5.1 illustrates some operations on data having an enumerated type.

```
program DayTime(Output);

   { Program 5.1 - Illustrate enumerated types. }

   type
      Days = (Mon, Tue, Wed, Thu, Fri, Sat, Sun);
      When = (Past, Present, Future);

   var
      Day: Days;
      Yesterday, Today, Tomorrow: Days;
      Time: When;

begin
   Today := Sun    { Pascal can't read a value of an
                      enumerated type from Input. };
   Time := Present;
   repeat
      if Time = Present then { Calculate Yesterday }
         begin  Time := Past;
            if Today = Mon then Yesterday := Sun
            else Yesterday := Pred(Today);
            Day := Yesterday
         end
      else
         if Time = Past then { Calculate Tomorrow }
            begin
               Time := Future;
               if Today = Sun then Tomorrow := Mon
               else Tomorrow := Succ(Today);
               Day := Tomorrow
            end
         else { Time = Future;  reset to Present }
            begin  Time := Present;
               Day := Today
            end;
      case Day of
         Mon: Write(Output, 'Monday');
         Tue: Write(Output, 'Tuesday');
         Wed: Write(Output, 'Wednesday');
         Thu: Write(Output, 'Thursday');
```

```
      Fri: Write(Output, 'Friday');
      Sat: Write(Output, 'Saturday');
      Sun: Write(Output, 'Sunday')
    end;
    Writeln(Output, Ord(Time) - 1)
  until Time = Present
end .
```

Produces as results:

```
Saturday    -1
Monday       1
Sunday       0
```

5.B. Subrange Types

A type may be defined as a *subrange* of any other previously defined ordinal type — called its *host type*. The definition of a subrange simply indicates the least and the largest constant value in the subrange, where the lower bound must not be greater than the upper bound. A subrange of the type Real is *not* allowed, because real is not an ordinal type.

Figure 5.b   Syntax diagram for *SubrangeType*

The host of the subrange type determines the validity of all operations involving values of the subrange type. Recall that ordinal-type assignment compatibility assumes that the variable and the expression are the same or subranges of the same ordinal type, and the value of the expression lies within the closed interval specified by the type of the variable. For example, given the declaration:

```
var A: 1..10; B: 0..30; C:20..30;
```

The host type for A, B, and C is Integer. Hence the assignments

```
A := B; C := B; B := C;
```

are all valid statements, although their execution may sometimes be an error. Whenever ordinal types are discussed throughout this text, the phrase "or subrange thereof" is therefore assumed to be implied and is not always mentioned.

Example:
```
type Days = (Mon,Tue,Wed,Thu,Fri,Sat,Sun) { enumerated type };
     Workdays = Mon..Fri { subrange of days };
     Index = 0..63 { subrange of Integer };
     Letter = 'A'..'Z' { subrange of Char };
     Natural = 0..MaxInt;
     Positive = 1..MaxInt;
```

Subrange types provide the means for a more explanatory statement of the problem. To the implementor they also suggest an opportunity to conserve memory space and to introduce validity checks upon assignment at run-time. (For an example with subrange types, see Program 6.1.). For example, a variable declared to be of type 0..200 might occupy only one byte (8 bits) on many implementations, whereas a variable of type Integer might occupy many bytes.

CHAPTER 6

Structured Types in General — The Array Type in Particular

Simple types (ordinal and real types) are unstructured types. The other types in Pascal are *structured types* and pointer types. As structured statements are compositions of other statements, structured types are compositions of other types. It is the type(s) of the *components* and — most importantly — the structuring method that characterize a structured type.

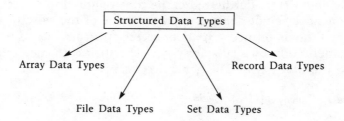

Figure 6.a   Type Taxonomy of Structured Data Types

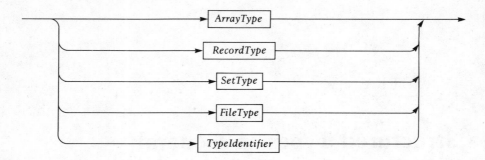

Figure 6.b Syntax diagram for *StructuredType*

An option available to each of the structuring methods is an indication of the preferred internal data representation. A structured type definition prefixed with the symbol packed signals the compiler to economize storage requirements, even at the expense of additional execution time and a possible expansion of the code, due to the necessary packing and unpacking operations. It is your responsibility to realize if you want this trade of execution efficiency for space. (The actual effects upon efficiency and savings in storage space are implementation dependent, and may, in fact, be nil.)

6.A. The Array Type

An array type consists of a fixed number of components (defined when the array type is introduced) all having the same type, called the *component type.* Each component can be explicitly denoted and directly accessed by the name of the array variable followed by the so-called *index* in square brackets. Indices are computable; their type is called the *index type.* Furthermore, the time required to select (access) a component does not depend upon the value of the selector (index); hence the array is termed a *random-access structure.*

The definition of a new array type specifies both the component type and the index type. The general form is:

```
type A = array [T1] of T2;
```

where A is a new type identifier; T1 is the index type, which must be ordinal, and T2 is any type.

Arrays provide a means of grouping under a single name several variables having identical characteristics. An array variable declaration gives a name to the entire array structure. Two operations valid for entire array variables are assignment and selection of components. A component is selected by specifying the name of the array variable followed by an ordinal expression enclosed in square brackets. The operations permitted on such a component variable are those which are valid for any variable of the component type of that array type.

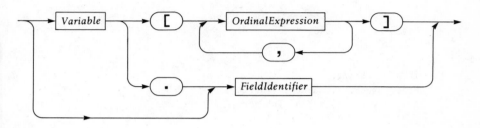

Figure 6.c   Syntax Diagram for *ComponentVariable*

Examples of variable declarations:
```
Memory: array [0..Max] of Integer
Sick: packed array [Days] of Boolean
```

Examples of sample assignments:
```
Memory[I+J] := X
Sick[Mon] := true
```

(Of course these examples assume the definition of the auxiliary identifiers.)

Programs 6.1 and 6.2 illustrate the use of arrays. Consider how you would extend Program 6.2 to plot more than one function — both with and without the use of an array.

Since T2 may be any type, the components of arrays may be structured. In particular, if T2 is also an array type, then the original array type A is said to be *multidimensional*. Hence, the declaration of a multidimensional array M can be so formulated:

```
var M: array [A..B] of array [C..D] of T;
```

and

```
M[I][J]
```

then denotes the component J (of type T) of component I of M.

```
program MinMax(Input,Output);

    { Program 6.1 - Find the largest and smallest number
                    in a given list. }

    const
       MaxSize = 20;

    type
       ListSize = 1..MaxSize;

    var
       Item: ListSize;
       Min, Max, First, Second: Integer;
       A: array [ListSize] of Integer;

begin
    for Item := 1 to MaxSize do
       begin  Read(Input, A[Item]);  Write(Output, A[Item] :4) end;
    Writeln(Output);

    Min := A[1];  Max := Min;  Item := 2;
    while Item < MaxSize do
       begin  First := A[Item];  Second := A[Item+1];
          if First > Second then
             begin
                if First > Max then Max := First;
                if Second < Min then Min := Second
             end
          else
             begin
                if Second > Max then Max := Second;
                if First < Min then Min := First
             end;
          Item := Item + 2
       end;
    if Item = MaxSize then
       if A[MaxSize] > Max then Max := A[MaxSize]
       else
          if A[MaxSize] < Min then Min := A[MaxSize];
    Writeln(Output, Max, Min)
end .
```

Produces as results:

```
 35  68  94   7  88  -5  -3  12  35   9  -6   3   0  -2  74  88  52  43   5   4

        94         -6
```

```
program Graph2(Output);

    { Program 6.2 - Generate graphic representation (with X-axis)
                of the function:
                    f(X) = exp(-X) * sin(2*Pi*X) . }

    const
        XLines = 16 { line spacings per 1 abscissa unit };
        Scale = 32  { character widths per 1 ordinate unit };
        ZeroY = 34  { character position of X axis };
        XLimit = 32 { length of graph in lines };
        YLimit = 68 { height of graph in character widths };

    type
        Domain = 1..YLimit;

    var
        Delta: Real { increment along abscissa };
        TwoPi: Real { 2 * Pi = 8 * ArcTan(1.0) };
        X, Y:  Real;
        Point: Integer;
        Plot, YPosition, Extent: Domain;
        YPlot: array [Domain] of Char;

begin  { initialize constants: }
    Delta := 1 / Xlines;
    TwoPi := 8 * ArcTan(1.0);

    for Plot := 1 to Ylimit do
        YPlot[Plot] := ' ';
    for Point := 0 to XLimit do
        begin
            X := Delta * Point;   Y := Exp(-X) * Sin(TwoPi * X);
            YPlot[ZeroY] := ':';
            YPosition := Round(Scale * Y) + ZeroY;
            YPlot[YPosition] := '*';
            if YPosition < ZeroY then Extent := ZeroY
            else Extent := YPosition;
            for Plot := 1 to Extent do Write(Output, YPlot[Plot]);
            Writeln(Output);   YPlot[YPosition] := ' '
        end
end .
```

Produces as results:

For multidimensional arrays, it is customary to make these convenient abbreviations:

```
var M: array [A..B,C..D] of T;
```

and

```
M[I,J]
```

We may regard M as a matrix and say that M[I,J] is component J (in column J) of component I of M (of row I of M).

Arrays are not limited to two dimensions, for T can again be a structured type. In general, the (abbreviated) form is:

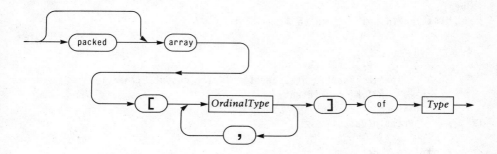

Figure 6.d Syntax diagram for *ArrayType*

If *n* index types are specified, the array is said to be *n-dimensional*, and a component is denoted by *n* index expressions.

If A and B are array variables of the same type, then the assignment statement

```
A := B
```

is allowed if the arrays are component-wise assignable:

```
A[i] := B[i]
```

(for each i that is a value of the index type), and is an abbreviation for the assignment of each corresponding component.

```
program MatrixMul(Input,Output);

    { Program 6.3 - Matrix Multiplication }

    const
        M = 4;  P = 3;  N = 2;

    var
        I: 1..M;
        J: 1..N;
        K: 1..P;
        Sum, Element: Integer;
        A: array [1..M, 1..P] of Integer;
        B: array [1..P, 1..N] of Integer;
        C: array [1..M, 1..N] of Integer;
begin
    { Assign initial values to A and B: }
    for I := 1 to M do
        begin
            for K := 1 to P do
                begin  Read(Input,Element);  Write(Output,Element);
                    A[I,K] := Element
                end;
            Writeln(Output)
        end;
    Writeln(Output);
    for K := 1 to P do
        begin
            for J := 1 to N do
                begin  Read(Input,Element);  Write(Output,Element);
                    B[K,J] := Element
                end;
            Writeln(Output)
        end;
    Writeln(Output);
    { Multiply A and B to get C: }
    for I := 1 to M do
        begin
            for J := 1 to N do
                begin  Sum := 0;
                    for K := 1 to P do
                        Sum := Sum + A[I,K] * B[K,J];
                    C[I,J] := Sum;  Write(Output,Sum)
                end;
            Writeln(Output)
        end;
    Writeln(Output)
end .
```

Produces as results:

```
   1        2        3
  -2        0        2
   1        0        1
  -1        2       -3


  -1        3
  -2        2
   2        1


   1       10
   6       -4
   1        4
  -9       -2
```

Note that the index types for arrays A, B, and C in the above program are fixed. If we could write a generalized matrix-multiply subprogram for a library, we need a facility to provide for adjustable index types. Pascal provides conformant-array parameters for this purpose (see Section 11.A.2); and Program 11.4, MatrixMul2, illustrates their use.

6.B.   String Types

Strings were defined earlier as sequences of characters enclosed in apostrophes (Section 1.E). Strings consisting of a single character are the constants of the standard type Char (Section 2.D); those of N characters (N > 1), are constants of a type defined by:

```
packed array [1..N] of Char
```

Such a type is called a *string type*.
   The assignment

```
A := E
```

where array variable A and expression E have any string types with the same number of components is valid. Similarly, the relational operators (=, <>, <, >, <=, and <=) may be used to compare any two strings that have the same number of components; the ordering considers the first element (A[1]) to be most significant and is determined by the ordering of the predeclared type Char.

6.C.   Pack and Unpack

Access to individual components of packed arrays is often costly, and depending on the situation and the particular Pascal implementation, sometimes you are advised to pack or unpack a packed array in a single operation. This is possible through the predeclared transfer procedures `Pack` and `Unpack`. Letting U be an unpacked array variable of type

```
array [A..D] of T { T cannot be a type containing a file type }
```

and P be a packed array variable of type

```
packed array [B..C] of T
```

where $ord(D) - ord(A) >= ord(C) - ord(B)$ then

```
Pack (U,I,P)
```

means to pack that part of U beginning at component I into P, and

```
Unpack (P,U,I)
```

means to unpack P into U beginning at component I.

CHAPTER 7

Record Types

The record types are perhaps the most flexible of data constructs. Conceptually, a record type is a template for a structure whose parts may have quite distinct characteristics. For example, assume we wish to record information about a person. Known are the name, height, sex, date of birth, number of dependents, and marital status. Furthermore, if the person is married or widowed, the date of the (last) marriage is given; if divorced, the date of the (most recent) divorce and whether this is the first divorce or not; and if single, no other information is of interest. All of this information can be expressed in a single "record," and each piece of information can be accessed separately.

7.A. Fixed Records

More formally, a record is a structure consisting of a fixed number of components, called *fields*. Unlike the array, components of a record type can have different types and cannot be indexed by an expression. A record-type definition specifies for each component its type and an identifier, the *field identifier*, to denote it. The scope of a field identifier is the innermost record in which it is defined. The two operations valid for entire record variables are assignment and selection of components.

In order that the type of selected component be evident from the program text (without executing the program), the record selector consists of fixed field identifiers rather than a computable index value.

To take a simple example, assume we wish to compute with complex numbers of the form a + bi, where a and b are real numbers and i is the square root of −1. There is no predefined type "complex." However, we can easily define a record type to represent complex numbers. This record would need two fields, both of type Real, for the real and imaginary parts. The syntax necessary to express this is:

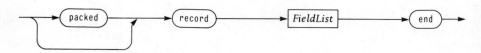

Figure 7.a   Syntax diagram for *RecordType*

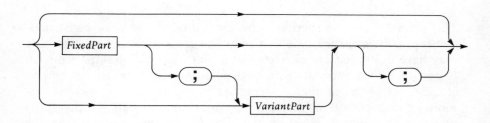

Figure 7.b   Syntax diagram for *FieldList*

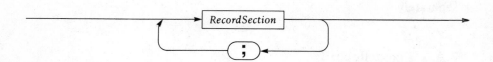

Figure 7.c   Syntax diagram for *FixedPart*

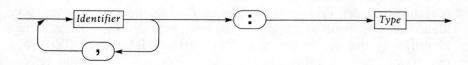

Figure 7.d   Syntax diagram for *RecordSection*

Applying these rules, we can state the following definition and declaration:

```
type Complex = record Re,Im: Real end;
var Z: Complex;
```

where `Complex` is a type identifier, `Re` and `Im` are identifiers of fields, and `Z` is a variable of type `Complex`. Consequently, `Z` is a record made up of two components or fields. See Program 7.1.

To access a record component, the name of the record is followed by a period, and the respective field identifier (see Figure 6.c). For example, the following assigns 5 + 3i to Z:

```
Z.Re := 5;
Z.Im := 3
```

Likewise, a type representing a date can be defined as:

```
Date = packed record
                Year: 1900..2100;
                Mo: (Jan, Feb, Mar, Apr, May, Jun,
                     Jul, Aug, Sep, Oct, Nov, Dec);
                Day: 1..31
             end
```

Note: The type `Date` also includes, for instance, a 31st April. A toy can be described as:

```
Toy = record
          Kind: (Ball, Top, Boat, Doll, Blocks,
                 Game, Model, Book);
          Cost: Real;
          Received: Date;
          Enjoyed: (Alot, Some, Alittle, None);
          Broken, Lost: Boolean
       end
```

A homework assignment can be defined as:

```
Assignment = packed record
                      Subject:(History, Language, Lit,
                               Math, Psych, Science);
                      Assigned: Date;
                      Grade: 0..4;
                      Weight: 1..10
                   end
```

```
program ComplexArithmetic(Output);

   { Program 7.1 - Illustrate operations on complex numbers. }

   const
      Increment = 4;

   type
      Complex =
         record
            Re, Im: Real
         end;

   var
      X, Y: Complex;
      Pair: Integer;
begin
   X.Re := 2;  X.Im := 5;   { initialize X }
   Y := X;                  { initialize Y }

   for Pair := 1 to 5 do
      begin
         Writeln(Output, 'X = ', X.Re :5:1, X.Im :5:1, 'i');
         Writeln(Output, 'Y = ', Y.Re :5:1, Y.Im :5:1, 'i');

         {X + Y}
         Writeln(Output, 'Sum = ', X.Re + Y.Re :5:1,
                     X.Im + Y.Im :5:1, 'i');

         {X * Y}
         Writeln(Output, 'Product = ', X.Re * Y.Re - X.Im*Y.Im :5:1,
                     X.Re * Y.Im + X.Im * Y.Re :5:1, 'i');
         Writeln(Output);

         X.Re := X.Re + Increment;
         X.Im := X.Im - Increment
      end
end .
```

Produces as results:

```
X =    2.0  5.0i
Y =    2.0  5.0i
Sum =    4.0 10.0i
Product = -21.0 20.0i

X =    6.0  1.0i
Y =    2.0  5.0i
Sum =    8.0  6.0i
Product =    7.0 32.0i
```

```
X =   10.0 -3.0i
Y =    2.0  5.0i
Sum =  12.0  2.0i
Product =  35.0 44.0i

X =   14.0 -7.0i
Y =    2.0  5.0i
Sum =  16.0 -2.0i
Product =  63.0 56.0i

X =   18.0-11.0i
Y =    2.0  5.0i
Sum =  20.0 -6.0i
Product =  91.0 68.0i
```

If the record is itself nested within another structure, the naming of the record variable reflects this structure. For example, assume we wish to record the most recent smallpox vaccination for each member in a family. A possibility is to define the members as an enumerated type, and then keep the dates in an array of records:

```
type FamilyMember = (Father, Mother, Childl, Childl, Child3);
var VaccinationDate: array [FamilyMember] of Date;
```

An update might then be recorded as:

```
VaccinationDate[Child3].Mo := Apr;
VaccinationDate[Child3].Day := 23;
VaccinationDate[Child3].Year := 1973
```

7.B.   Variant Records

Sometimes we may want to include information in a record structure which depends on some of the other information already in the record. We can define a variant record type which includes additional fields depending on the value of another field.

The syntax for a record type makes provisions for a *variant part*, implying that a record type may be specified as consisting of several *variants*. This means that different variables, although said to be of the same type, may assume structures which differ in the number and types of components.

Each variant is characterized by a list, in parentheses, of declarations of its pertinent components. Each list is preceded by one or more constants, and the set of lists is preceded by a case clause specifying the data type of these constants (i.e., the type according to which the variants are discriminated).

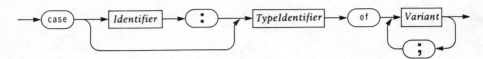

Figure 7.e   Syntax diagram for *VariantPart*

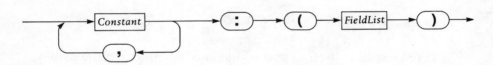

Figure 7.f   Syntax diagram for *Variant*

As an example, assume the existence of a

```
type MaritalStatus = (Married, Widowed, Divorced, Single)
```

Then we can describe persons by data of the

```
type Person =
    record
        { fields common to all persons go here };
        case MaritalStatus of
            Married: ( { fields of married persons only } );
            Single: ( { fields of single persons only } );
            ...
    end
```

Note that *every* value of the type by which the variants are discriminated (the so-called *tag type*) must be explicitly listed with one of the variants. Thus in the above example the constants Widowed and Divorced must also appear (along with Married and Single) for the example to be valid.

Usually, a component (field) of the record itself indicates its currently valid variant. For example, the above defined person record is likely to contain a common field

```
MS: MaritalStatus
```

This frequent situation can be abbreviated by including the declaration of the discriminating component — the so-called *tag field* — in the case clause itself, i.e., by writing

```
case MS: MaritalStatus of
```

It is helpful to "outline" the information about a person before defining it as a variant record structure.

   I. Person
      A. name (last, first)
      B. height (natural number)
      C. sex (male, female)
      D. date of birth (year, month, day)
      E. number of dependents (natural number)
      F. marital status
         if married,widowed
            a. date of marriage (year, month, day)
         if divorced
            a. date of divorce (year, month, day)
            b. first divorce (false, true)
         if single

Figure 7.g is a corresponding picture of two "sample" people with different attributes.

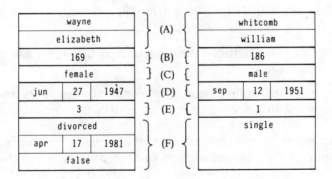

Figure 7.g Two Sample People

A record defining `Person` can now be formulated as:

```
type String15 = packed array [1..15] of Char;
     Status = (Married, Widowed, Divorced, Single);
     Date = packed record
                     Year: 1900..2100;
                     Mo: (Jan, Feb, Mar, Apr, May, Jun,
                          Jul, Aug, Sep, Oct, Nov, Dec);
                     Day: 1..31;
                 end;
     Natural = 0..MaxInt;
     Person = record
                 Name: record First, Last: String15 end;
                 Height: Natural { centimeters };
                 Sex: (Male, Female);
                 Birth: Date;
                 Depdts: Natural
                 case MS: Status of
                     Married, Widowed: (MDate: Date);
                     Divorced: (DDate: Date;
                                    FirstD: Boolean);
                     Single: ()
             end { Person };
```

Notes:

1. All field names must be distinct — even if they occur in different variants.

2. If a variant is empty (i.e., has no fields), the form is:
   C: ( )

3. A field list can have only one variant part and it must follow the fixed part of the record.

4. A variant may itself contain a variant part; hence variant parts can be nested.

5. The scope of enumerated type constant identifiers that are introduced in a record type extends over the enclosing block.

Referencing a record component is essentially a simple linear reconstruction of the outline. As an example, assume a variable P of type `Person` and "create" the second of the model people.

```
P.Name.Last := 'Whitcomb      ';
P.Name.First := 'William       ';
```

```
P.Height := 186;
P.Sex := Male;
P.Birth.Year := 1951;
P.Birth.Mo := Sep;
P.Birth.Day := 12;
P.Depdts := 1;
P.MS := Single;
```

7.C.   The With Statement

The above notation can be a bit tedious, and you may wish to abbreviate it using the *with statement*. The with statement effectively opens the scope containing the field identifiers of the specified record variable, so that the field identifiers may occur as variable identifiers (thereby providing an opportunity for the Pascal compiler to optimize the qualified statement). The general form is:

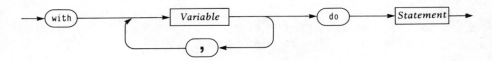

Figure 7.h   Syntax diagram for *WithStatement*

Within the qualified statement of the with statement we denote a field of a record variable by designating only its field identifier (without preceding it with the notation of the entire record variable).

The with statement below is equivalent to the preceding series of assignments:

```
with P do
    begin
        with Name do
            begin Last := 'Whitcomb        ';
                First := 'William        '
            end;
        Height := 186;
        Sex := Male;
        with Birth do
            begin Year := 1951; Mo := Sep; Day := 12 end;
        Depdts := 1;
        MS := Single;
    end
```

Likewise,

```
var CurrentDate: Date;
...
with Currentdate do
   if Mo = Dec then
      begin Mo := Jan; Year := Year + 1 end
   else Mo := succ(Mo)
```

is equivalent to

```
var CurrentDate: Date;
...
if CurrentDate.Mo = Dec then
   begin CurrentDate.Mo := Jan;
      CurrentDate.Year := CurrentDate.Year + 1 end
else CurrentDate.Mo := succ(CurrentDate.Mo)
```

And the following accomplishes the vaccine update example given earlier:

```
with VaccinationDate[Child3] do
   begin Year := 1973; Mo := Apr; Day := 23 end
```

When the with statement is executed, a reference to the record variable is established prior to the execution of the qualified statement. Therefore assignments made by the qualified statement to any elements of the record variable list will not change the identity of the record variable.

For example:
```
var Who: FamilyMember;
...
Who := Father;
with VaccinationDate[Who] do
   begin
      Who := Mother;
      Mo := Jul; Day := 7; Year := 1947
   end
```

The with statement sets the fields of VaccinationDate[Father].
Nested with statements can be abbreviated. The form:

```
with R1, R2, ..., Rn do S
```

is equivalent to

```
with R1 do
   with R2 do
      ...
         with Rn do S
```

Thus the previous example defining a person P could be rewritten:

```
with P, Name, Birth do
   begin Last := 'Whitcomb          ';
      First := 'William          ';
      Height := 186;
      Sex := Male;
      Year := 1951;
      Mo := Sep;
      Day := 12;
      Depdts := 1;
      MS := Single;
   end { with }
```

An example which illustrates scopes of field identifiers follows.
Whereas:

```
var A: array [2..8] of Integer;
    A: 2..8;
```

is not allowed, because the definition of A is ambiguous,

```
var A: Integer;
    B: record A: Real; B: Boolean
       end;
```

is allowed, because the notation for the integer A is easily distinguishable from the real B.A. Likewise, the record variable B is distinguishable
from the Boolean B.B. Within the qualified statement S in

```
with B do S
```

the identifiers A and B now denote the components B.A and B.B
respectively, and the integer variable identified by A is inaccessible.

CHAPTER 8

Set Types

A set type provides a compact structure for recording information about the existence or combination of a collection of values having the same ordinal type. More precisely, a set type defines the set of values that is the powerset of its base type, i.e., the set of all possible subsets of values of the base type, including the empty set. Therefore, a single value of a set type is a set, and the elements of that set are values of the base type. A set is also a random-access structure whose elements all have the same base type, which must be an ordinal type.

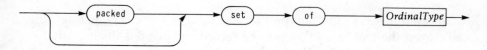

Figure 8.a   Syntax diagram for *SetType*

Operations valid for entire set values are assignment, the familiar set operations (e.g., set union), equality, and selection of components by testing for membership (see below). Set values may be built up from set elements by the operation of set construction. Implementations of Pascal usually define limits for the size of sets, which can be quite small (e.g., the number bits in a machine "word"). The limit applies directly to the range of the base type of the set type.

8.A.   Set Constructors

A set value can be specified by a set constructor which contains descriptions of the set elements separated by commas and enclosed in square brackets. An element description can be an expression, the value of which is the element, or a range of the form low..high, where the values of the expressions low and high are the lower and upper bounds of a collection of elements. If the lower bound is greater than the upper bound of the range (i.e., low > high), no elements are described.

The expressions must all have the same ordinal type which is the *base type* of the set constructor type. The set constructor [] denotes the empty set of *every* set type. Set constructors do not carry full type information [see Reference 10], such as whether or not the set is packed. Therefore the type of a set constructor is both packed and unpacked to be type compatible with other sets in set expressions.

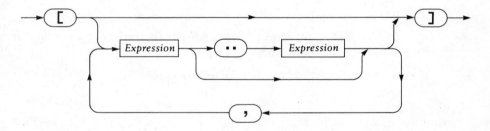

Figure 8.b   Syntax diagram for *SetConstructor*

Examples of set constructors:
```
[13]
[i+j,i-j]
['0'..'9']
['a','b','c','d','e','f','g','h','i','j','k','l','m','n','o',
 'p','q','r','s','t','u','v','w','x','y','z']
```

8.B.   Set Operations

If X is a set variable, and E is a set expression, then

```
X := E
```

is allowed if all members of E are in the base type of X, and the types of X and E both are packed or neither is packed. The following operators are applicable on all objects with set structure. Assume A and B are set expressions of the same type:

A + B   set union of all elements in both A and B.

A * B   set intersection of all elements common to both A and B.

A − B   set difference of all elements of A that are not also elements of B.

Five relational operators are applicable to set operands. Assume A and B are set expressions of the same type and e is an ordinal expression of the base type.

e in A   set membership. The result is true when e is an element of A, otherwise false.

A = B   set equality.

A <> B   set inequality.

A <= B   set inclusion; true if A is a proper or improper subset of B.

A >= B   set inclusion; true if B is a proper or improper subset of A.

Examples of declarations
```
type Primary = (Red, Yellow, Blue);
     Color = set of Primary;
var Hue1, Hue2: Color;
   Vowels, Consonants, Letters: set of Char;
   Opcode: set of 0..7;
      Add: Boolean;
      Ch: Char;
```

Examples of assignments
```
Hue1 := [Red]; Hue2 := [];
Hue2 := Hue2 + [succ(Red)]

Letters := ['A','B','C','D','E','F','G','H','I',
           'J','K','L','M','N','O','P','Q','R',
           'S','T','U','V','W','X','Y','Z'];
Vowels := ['A','E','I','O',U];
Consonants := Letters − Vowels

Add := [2,3] <= Opcode
```

Set operations are intended to be relatively fast and can be used to eliminate more complicated tests. A simpler test for:

```
if (Ch='A')or(Ch='E')or(Ch='I')or(Ch='O')or(Ch='U') then S
```

is:

```
if Ch in ['A','E','I','O','U'] then S
```

```
program Convert(Input,Output);

    { Program 8.1 - Read a sequence of digits and convert them to the
                    integer they represent. Assume no leading sign. }

    var
        Ch: Char;
        Digits: set of '0'..'9';
        Number: Integer;

begin
    Digits := ['0'..'9']  { initialize value of the set };
    Read(Input, Ch);
    Number := 0;
    while Ch in Digits do
        begin
            Number := Number * 10 + Ord(Ch) - Ord('0');
            Writeln(Output, Number);
            Read(Input, Ch)
        end
    { Ch contains the character following the integer }
end .
```

Produces as results:

```
   4
  43
 432
4321
```

```
program SetOperations(Output);

   { program 8.2 - Illustrate set operations. }

   type
      Days = (Mon, Tue, Wed, Thu, Fri, Sat, Sun);
      Week = set of Days;

   var
      FullWeek, Work, Free: Week;
      Day: Days;

   procedure Check(W: Week); { procedures are introduced in Chapter 11 }

      var D: Days;

   begin
      for D := Mon to Sun do
         if D in W then Write(Output, 'x') else Write(Output, 'o');
      Writeln(Output)
   end { Check };

begin
   Work:= [];  Free := [];  FullWeek := [Mon..Sun];
   Day := Sat;
   Free := [Day] + Free + [Sun];
   Check(Free);
   Work := FullWeek - Free;
   Check(Work);
   if Free <= FullWeek then Write(Output, 'O');
   if FullWeek >= Work then Write(Output, 'K');
   if not (Work >= Free) then Write(Output, ' Jack');
   if [Sat] <= Work then Write(Output, 'Forget it!');
   Writeln(Output)
end .
```

Produces as results:

```
oooooxx
xxxxxoo
OK Jack
```

8.C.   On Program Development

Programming — in the sense of designing and formulating algorithms and data structures — is in general a complicated process requiring the mastery of numerous details and specific techniques. Only in exceptional cases will there be a single good solution. Usually, so many solutions exist that the choice of an optimal program requires a thorough analysis not only of the available algorithms and computer systems but also of the way in which the program will most frequently be used.

Consequently, the construction of a program should consist of a sequence of deliberations, investigations, and design decisions. In the early stages, attention is best concentrated on the global problems, and the first draft of a solution may pay little attention to details. As the design process progresses, we can split the problem into subproblems, and gradually give more consideration to the details of problem specification and to the characteristics of the available tools. The terms *stepwise refinement* [Reference 2] and *structured programming* [Reference 4] are associated with this approach.

The remainder of this chapter illustrates the development of a program by rewording (to be consistent with Pascal notation) an example C.A.R. Hoare presents in the book *Structured Programming* [Reference 4, "Notes on Data Structuring"].

The problem is to generate the prime numbers falling in the range 2. .n, where n >= 2. After a comparison of the various algorithms, that of Eratosthenes' sieve is chosen because of its simplicity (no multiplications or divisions).

The first formulation is verbal.

1. Put all the numbers between 2 and n into the "sieve."

2. Select and remove the smallest number remaining in the sieve.

3. Include this number in the "primes."

4. Step through the sieve, removing all multiples of this number.

5. If the sieve is not empty, repeat steps 2–5.

Although initialization of variables is the first step in the execution of a program, it is often the last in the development process. Full comprehension of the algorithm is a prerequisite for making the proper initializations; updating of these initializations with each program modification is necessary to keep the program running. (Unfortunately, updating is not always sufficient!).

Hoare chooses a set type with elements 2..n to represent both the sieve and the primes. The following is a slight variation of the program sketch he presents.

```
program Prime1;

   { Program 8.3 - Use sets to implement Sieve of Erastosthenes. }

   const
      N = 10000;

   type
      Positive = 1..MaxInt;

   var
      Sieve, Primes: set of 2..N;
      NextPrime, Multiple: Positive;

begin { initialize }
   Sieve := [2..N];  Primes := [];  NextPrime := 2;
   repeat  { find next prime }
      while not (NextPrime in Sieve) do NextPrime := Succ(NextPrime);
      Primes := Primes + [NextPrime];
      Multiple := NextPrime;
      while Multiple <= N do { eliminate }
         begin  Sieve := Sieve - [Multiple];
            Multiple := Multiple + NextPrime;
         end
   until Sieve = []
end .
```

As an exercise Hoare proposes rewriting the program, so that the sets only represent the odd numbers. The following is one solution. Note the close correlation with the first solution.

```
program Prime2;

   { Program 8.4 - Use sets to implement Sieve of Erastosthenes;
                   represent odd numbers only. }
```

```
const
    N = 5000  { N' = N div 2 };

type
    Positive = 1..MaxInt;

var
    Sieve, Primes: set of 2..N;
    NextPrime, Multiple, NewPrime: Positive;
begin { initialize }
    Sieve := [2..N];  Primes := [];  NextPrime := 2;
    repeat { find next prime }
        while not (NextPrime in Sieve) do NextPrime := Succ(NextPrime);
        Primes := Primes + [NextPrime];
        NewPrime := 2 * NextPrime - 1;
        Multiple := NextPrime;
        while Multiple <= N do { eliminate }
            begin  Sieve := Sieve - [Multiple];
                Multiple := Multiple + NextPrime;
            end
    until Sieve = []
end .
```

A design goal for Pascal implementations is that all basic set operations execute relatively fast. Some implementations restrict the maximum size of sets according to their "wordlength," so that each element of the base set is represented by one bit (0 meaning absence, 1 meaning presence). Most implementations would not accept a set with 10,000 elements. These considerations lead to an adjustment in the data representation, as shown in Program 8.5.

A large set can be represented as an array of smaller sets such that each "fits" into a few words (implementation dependent). The following program uses the second sketch as an abstract model of the algorithm. Sieve and Primes are redefined as arrays of sets; Next is defined as a record.

```
program Prime3(Output);

{ Program 8.5 - Generate the primes between 3..10000 using
                a sieve containing odd integers in this range. }
```

```
const
    SetSize = 128 { implementation dependent };
    MaxElement = 127;
    Setparts = 39 { = 10000 div Setsize div 2 };

type
    Natural = 0..MaxInt;

var
    Sieve, Primes:
        array [0..SetParts] of
            set of 0..MaxElement;
    NextPrime:
        record
            Part, Element: Natural
        end;
    Multiple, NewPrime: Natural;
    P, N, Count: Natural;
    Empty: Boolean;

begin { initialize }
    for P := 0 to SetParts do
        begin  Sieve[P] := [0 .. MaxElement];  Primes[P] := []  end;
    Sieve[0] := Sieve[0] - [0];  Empty := False;
    NextPrime.Part := 0;  NextPrime.Element := 1;

    with NextPrime do
        repeat { find next prime }
            while not (Element in Sieve[Part]) do Element := Succ(Element);
            Primes[Part] := Primes[Part] + [Element];
            NewPrime := 2 * Element + 1;
            Multiple := Element;  P := Part;
            while P <= SetParts do { eliminate }
               begin  Sieve[P] := Sieve[P] - [Multiple];
                   P := P + Part * 2;
                   Multiple := Multiple + NewPrime;
                   while Multiple > MaxElement do
                       begin  P := P + 1;
                           Multiple := Multiple - SetSize
                       end
               end;
            if Sieve[Part] = [] then
                begin  Empty := True;  Element := 0  end;
            while Empty and (Part < SetParts) do
                begin
                    Part := Part + 1;  Empty := Sieve[Part] = []
                end
        until Empty;
```

```
Count := 0;
for P := 0 to SetParts do
   for N := 0 to MaxElement do
      if N in Primes[P] then
         begin
            Write(Output, 2 * N + 1 + P * SetSize * 2:6);
            Count := Count + 1;
            if (Count mod 8) = 0 then Writeln(Output)
         end
end.
```

Produces as results:

```
  3      5      7     11     13     17     19     23
 29     31     37     41     43     47     53     59
 61     67     71     73     79     83     89     97
101    103    107    109    113    127    131    137


         .      .      .      .      .      .      .
         .      .      .      .      .      .      .
         .      .      .      .      .      .      .


9871   9883   9887   9901   9907   9923   9929   9931
9941   9949   9967   9973  10007  10009  10037  10039
10061  10067  10069  10079  10091  10093  10099  10103
10111  10133  10139  10141  10151  10159  10163  10169
```

CHAPTER 9

File Types

In many ways the simplest structuring method is the sequence. In the data-processing profession the generally accepted term to describe a sequence is a *sequential file*. Pascal uses simply the word *file* to specify a structure consisting of a sequence of components — all of which have the same type. A special kind of file called a textfile consists of a sequence of variable-length lines of characters and forms the basis for legible communications between people and computer systems.

9.A. The File Structure

A natural ordering of the components is defined through the sequence, and at any instance only one component is directly accessible. The other components are accessible by progressing sequentially through the file. The number of components, called the *length* of the file, is not fixed by the file-type definition. This is a characteristic which clearly distinguishes the file from the array. A file with no components is said to be *empty*. A file type, therefore, differs from array, record, and set types because it is a sequential-access structure whose components all have the same type.

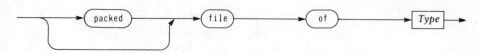

Figure 9.a   Syntax diagram for *FileType*

The declaration of every file variable F automatically introduces a *buffer variable*, denoted by F↑, of the component type. It can be considered as an access to the file through which one can either inspect (read) the value of existing components or generate (write) new components, and which is automatically advanced by certain file operations. Assignment is not possible to entire file variables. Rather the buffer variable is used to append components one at a time, in a one-way (sequential) manner. The buffer variable becomes undefined when the file is positioned past its last component.

Figure 9.b   Syntax diagram for *BufferVariable*

The sequential processing, varying length, and the existence of a buffer variable suggest that files may be associated with *secondary storage* and *peripherals*. Exactly how the components are allocated is implementation dependent, but we assume that only some of the components are present in primary storage at any one time, and only the component indicated by F↑ is directly accessible.

When the buffer variable F↑ is moved beyond the end of a file F, the predeclared Boolean function eof(F) returns the value true, otherwise false. The basic file-handling procedures are:

Reset(F)   initiates inspection (reading) of F by placing the file at its beginning. If F is not empty, the value of the first component of F is assigned to F↑ and eof(F) becomes false.

Rewrite(F)   initiates generation (writing) of the file F. The current value of F is replaced with the empty file. Eof(F) becomes true, and a new file may be written.

Get(F)   advances the file to the next component and assigns
                the value of this component to the buffer variable
                F↑. If no next component exists, then eof(F) becomes
                true, and F↑ becomes undefined. The effect of Get(F)
                is an error if eof(F) is true prior to its execution or
                if F is being generated.

Put(F)   appends the value of the buffer variable F↑ to the
                file F. The effect is an error unless prior to execu-
                tion the predicate eof(F) is true. eof(F) remains
                true, and F↑ becomes undefined. Put(F) is an error if
                F is being inspected.

In principle, all the operations of sequential-file generation and inspection can be expressed entirely in terms of the four primitive file
operators and the predicate eof. In practice, it is often natural to
combine the operation of advancing the file position with the access
to the buffer variable. We therefore introduce the two procedures Read
and Write as follows:

Read(F,X) (for X a variable) is equivalent to

```
begin
   X := F↑; Get(F)
end
```

Write(F,E) (for E an expression) is equivalent to

```
begin
   F↑ := E; Put(F)
end
```

Read and Write are in fact special procedures extended to accept a
variable number of actual parameters (V1...Vn are variables and E1...En
are expressions):

Read(F,V1,...,Vn) is equivalent to the statement

```
begin Read(F,V1);...;Read(F,Vn) end
```

and

Write(F,E1,...,En) is equivalent to the statement

```
begin Write(F,E1);...;Write(F,En) end
```

The advantage of using these procedures lies not only in brevity, but
also in conceptual simplicity, since the existence of a buffer variable

F↑, which is sometimes undefined, may be ignored. The buffer varia-ble may, however, be useful as a "lookahead" device.

Examples of declarations
```
var Data: file of Integer;
    A: Integer;

var Plotfile: file of
                record
                     C: Color;
                     Len: Natural
                end;

var Club: file of Person;
    P: Person;
```

Examples of statements with files
```
A := Data↑; Get(Data)

Read(Data,A)

Plotfile↑.C := Red;
Plotfile↑.Len := 17;  Put(Plotfile)

Club↑ := P;  Put(Club)

Write(Club,P)
```

Files may be local to a program (or local to a procedure), or they may already exist outside the program. The latter are called *external files*. External files are passed as parameters in the program heading (see Chapter 3) into the program.

The next two programs illustrate the use of files. Program 9.1 reprocesses a file of real numbers representing measurements produced by an instrument or another program. Program 9.2 operates on two files representing sequences of persons ordered by last name.

```
F1,F2, ... , Fm    and    G1,G2, ... ,Gn
```

such that $F(I+1) >= F(I)$ and $G(J+1) >= G(J)$, for all I,J and *merges* them into one ordered file H such that

```
H(K+1) >= H(K)  for K = 1,2, ... ,(M+N-1).
```

9.B. Textfiles

Textfiles are files that consist of a sequence of characters that is subdivided into variable-length *lines*. The predefined type Text is used to declare textfiles.

```pascal
program Normalize(DataIn, DataOut);

   { Program 9.1 - Normalize a file of measurements generated as
                   real numbers from an instrument or another
                   program. }

   type
      Measurements = file of Real;
      Natural = 0..MaxInt;

   var
      DataIn, DataOut: Measurements;
      Sum, Mean,
      SumOfSquares, StandardDeviation: Real;
      N: Natural;

begin
   Reset(DataIn);   N := 0;
   Sum := 0.0;   SumOfSquares := 0.0;

   while not eof(DataIn) do
      begin   N := N + 1;
         Sum := Sum + DataIn↑;
         SumOfSquares := SumOfSquares + Sqr(DataIn↑);
         Get(DataIn)
      end;
   Mean := Mean / N;
   StandardDeviation := Sqrt( (SumOfSquares / N) - Sqr(Mean) );
   Reset(DataIn);   Rewrite(DataOut);
   while not Eof(DataIn) do
      begin
         DataOut↑ := (DataIn↑ - Mean) / StandardDeviation;
         Put(DataOut);   Get(DataIn)
      end
end { Normalize }.
```

```pascal
program MergeFiles(F,G,H);

    { Program 9.2 - Merge files F and G sorted by
                    last name into H. }

    type
        Natural = 0..MaxInt;
        String15 = packed array [1..15] of Char;
        Person =  record
                        Name:
                            record
                                First, Last: String15;
                            end;
                        Height: Natural { centimeters } ;
                    end;

    var
        F, G, H: file of Person;
        EndFG: Boolean;

begin
    Reset(F);  Reset(G);  Rewrite(H);
    EndFG := Eof(F) or Eof(G);
    while not EndFG do
        begin
            if F↑.Name.Last < G↑.Name.Last then
                begin  H↑ := F↑;  Get(F);  EndFG := Eof(F)
                end
            else
                begin  H↑ := G↑;  Get(G);  EndFG := Eof(G)
                end;
            Put(H)
        end;
    while not Eof(G) do
        begin
            Write(H, G↑);  Get(G)
        end;
    while not Eof(F) do
        begin
            Write(H, F↑);  Get(F)
        end
end .
```

We may consider the type Text as being defined over the base type Char extended by a (hypothetical) line terminator or end-of-line marker. Therefore type Text is *not* equivalent to (Packed) file of Char. This end-of-line marker can be both recognized and generated by the following special textfile procedures.

Writeln(F)   terminate the current line of the textfile F.

Readln(F)   skip to the beginning of the next line of the textfile F (F↑ becomes the first character of the next line).

Eoln(F)   a Boolean function indicating whether the end of the current line in the textfile F has been reached. (If true, F↑ corresponds to the position of a line separator, but F↑ is a *blank*.)

If F is a textfile and Ch a character variable, the following abbreviated notation may be used.

abbreviated form	expanded form
Write(F,Ch)	F↑ := Ch; Put(F)
Read(F,Ch)	Ch := F↑; Get(F)

Input and Output are the names of two standard textfile variables used as program parameters for legible reading and writing of text. Chapter 12 describes them in detail together with extended forms of the procedures Read, Write, Readln, and Writeln.

The following program schemata use the above conventions to demonstrate some typical operations performed on textfiles.

1. Writing a textfile Y. Assume that P(C) computes a (next) character and assigns it to parameter C. If the current line is to be terminated, a Boolean variable B1 is set to true; and if the text is to be terminated, B2 is set to true.

```
Rewrite(Y);
repeat
   repeat P(C); Write(Y,C)
   until B1;
   Writeln(Y)
until B2
```

2. Reading a textfile X. Assume that Q(C) denotes the processing of a (next) character C. R denotes an action to be executed upon encountering the end of a line.

```
Reset(X);
while not eof(X) do
    begin
        while not eoln(X) do
            begin Read(X,C); Q(C)
            end;
        R; Readln(X)
    end
```

3. Copying a textfile X to a textfile Y while preserving the line structure of X.

```
Reset(X); Rewrite(Y);
While not eof(X) do
    begin { copy a line }
        while not eoln(X) do
            begin Read(X,C); Write(Y,C)
            end;
        Readln(X); Writeln(Y)
    end
```

A note on implementation: A straightforward method of representing the end-of-line marker is by using control characters. For instance, in the ASCII character set the two characters cr (carriage return) and lf (line feed) conventionally are used to mark the end of a line. However, some computer systems use a character set devoid of such control characters; this implies that other methods for indicating the end of a line must be employed.

CHAPTER 10

Pointer Types

So far we have talked about types that provide for the declaration of statically allocated variables. A *static variable* is one that is declared in a program and subsequently denoted by its identifier. It is called static, because it exists (i.e., memory is allocated for it) during the entire execution of the block (program, procedure, or function) to which it is local. A variable may, on the other hand, be created and destroyed *dynamically* during the execution of a block (without any correlation to the static structure of the program). Such a variable is consequently called a *dynamic variable* or an *identified variable*.

10.A. Pointer Variables and Identified (Dynamic) Variables

Identified (dynamic) variables do not occur in an explicit variable declaration and cannot be accessed directly by identifiers. Instead they are created and destroyed by using the predeclared procedures New and Dispose, and they are identified by pointer values (which may be implemented as nothing more than the storage addresses of the newly allocated variables). Pointer values must be assigned to previously existing pointer variables having the appropriate pointer type.

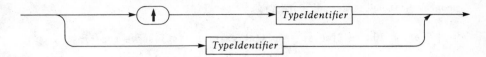

Figure 10.a   Syntax diagram for *PointerType*

The description of a pointer type P specifies a *domain type* T:

    type P = ↑T;

The set of pointer values of type P consists of an unbounded number of *identifying values*, each of which identifies a variable of type T, together with the special value nil that does not identify any variable.

An identified (dynamic) variable is accessed by the pointer value that identifies it; in particular, if Ptr is declared as:

    var Ptr: P;

and an identifying value has been assigned to Ptr, then the construct Ptr↑ is used to denote the identified variable.

Figure 10.b   Syntax diagram for *IdentifiedVariable*

Ptr↑ is an error if Ptr is nil or undefined.

Use New(Ptr) to create or allocate an identified variable of type T and to assign its identifying value to Ptr. Use Dispose(Ptr) to destroy or deallocate the variable identified by the value of Ptr; Ptr becomes undefined after Dispose.

Pointers are a simple tool for the construction of complicated and flexible (and even recursive) data structures. If the type T is a record structure that contains one or more fields of type P, then structures equivalent to arbitrary finite graphs may be built, where the identified variables represent the nodes, and the pointers are the edges.

Program 10.1 illustrates the use of pointers to maintain a waiting list of clients. (Procedures are discussed in the next chapter.)

```pascal
program WaitingList(Input,Output);

   { Program 10.1 - Simulate a client waiting list; serve the first 3. }

   const
      NameLength = 15;

   type
      NameIndex = 1..NameLength;
      NameString= packed array [NameIndex] of Char;
      Natural = 0..MaxInt;
      ClientPointer = ↑Client;
      Client =
         record
            Name: NameString;
            Nxt: ClientPointer
         end;

   var
      Head, Tail: ClientPointer;
      Name: packed array [NameIndex] of Char;

   procedure ReadName;
      var
         c: NameIndex;
   begin
      for c := 1 to NameLength do
         if Eoln(Input) then Name[c] := ' '
         else
            begin  Read(Input,Name[c]);  Write(Output,Name[c])  end;
      Readln(Input);  Writeln(Output)
   end { ReadName };

   procedure AddClientToList;
      var
         NewClient: ClientPointer;
   begin
      New(NewClient);
      if Head = nil then Head := NewClient
      else Tail↑.Nxt := NewClient;
      NewClient↑.Name := Name;  NewClient↑.Nxt := nil;
      Tail := NewClient
   end { AddClientToList };
```

```
    procedure ServeClient(HowMany: Natural);
       var
           ClientToServe: ClientPointer;
    begin
       while (HowMany > 0) and (Head <> nil) do
           begin  ClientToServe := Head;  Head := Head↑.Nxt;
               Writeln(ClientToServe↑.Name); Dispose(ClientToServe);
               HowMany := HowMany - 1
           end
    end { ServeClients };
begin { WaitingList }
   Head := nil;
   while not Eof(Input) do
      begin  ReadName;  AddClientToList  end;
   Writeln(Output);
   ServeClients(3)
end { WaitingList } .
```

Produces as results:

```
Hikita
Balasubramanyam
Nagel
Lecarme
Bello
Pokrovsky
Barron
Yuen
Sale
Price

Hikita
Balasubramanyam
Nagel
```

As another example, consider the construction of a "data base" for a given group of people. Assume the persons are represented by records as defined in Chapter 7. We may then form a chain or linked list of such records by adding a field of a pointer type and use the list for searching and insertion operations:

```
type Link = ↑Person;
    ...
    Person = record
               ...
               Next: Link;
               ...
           end;
```

A linked list of n persons can be represented as in Figure 10.c. Each box represents one person.

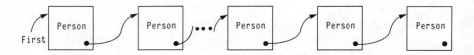

Figure 10.c   Linked List

A variable of type Link, called First, points to the first person of the list. The Next field of the last person in the list is nil. Note in passing that

```
First↑.Next↑.Next
```

points to the third person in the list.

If we assume that, for example, we can read integer data representing the heights of people, then the following code could have been used to construct the above chain.

```
var First, P: Link; H,I: Integer;
          . . .
First := nil
for I := 1 to N do
   begin Read(H); New(P);
      P↑.Next := First;
      P↑.Height := H; InitializeOtherFields(P↑);
      First := P
   end
```

Note that the list grows backwards. For purposes of access, we will introduce another variable, say Pt, of type Link and allow it to move freely through the list. To demonstrate selection, we assume there is a Person with Height equal to 175 and access this Person. The strategy is to advance Pt via Link until the desired person is located:

```
Pt := First;
while Pt↑.Height <> 175 do Pt := Pt↑.Next
```

In words this says, "Let Pt point to the first person. While the height of the person pointed to (identified) by Pt is not 175, assign to Pt the pointer value stored in the Next field (also a pointer variable) of the record that Pt currently identifies."

This simple search statement works only if one is sure that there is at least one person with Height equal to 175 on the list. But is this realistic? A check for failing to find 175 before reaching the end of the list is mandatory unless you can guarantee it. We might first try the following solution:

```
Pt := First;
while (Pt <> nil) and (Pt↑.Height <> 175) do
    Pt := Pt↑.Next
```

But recall Section 4.A. If Pt = nil, the variable Pt↑, referenced in the second factor of the termination condition, *does not exist* at all, and is an error. The following are two possible solutions which treat this situation correctly:

```
(1)  Pt:= First; B := true;
     while (Pt <> nil) and B do
     if Pt↑.Height = 175 then B := false else Pt := Pt↑.Next

(2)  Pt := First;
     while Pt <> nil do
         begin if Pt↑.Height = 175 then goto 13;
             Pt := Pt↑.Next
         end;
     13:
```

10.B. New and Dispose

To pose another problem, say we wish to add the sample person to the data base. First a variable must be allocated, and its identifying value obtained by means of the predeclared procedure New.

New(P)	a procedure that allocates a new identified (dynamic) variable P↑ having as its type the domain type of P, and creates a new identifying pointer value having the type possessed by P and assigns it to P. If P↑ is a variant record, New(P) allocates enough space to accommodate all variants.
New(P,C1,...,Cn)	allocates a new identified (dynamic) variable P↑ having the variant record type of P with tag field values C1,...,Cn for n nested variant parts, and creates a new identifying pointer value having the type possessed by P and assigns it to P.

Warning: if a record variable P↑ is created by the second form of New, then this variable must not change its variant during program execution. Assignment to the entire variable is an error; however one can assign to the components of P↑.

The first step in programming a solution to our problem posed above, is to introduce a pointer variable. Let it be called NewP. Then the statement

```
New(NewP)
```

will allocate a new variable of type Person.

In the next step the new variable, referenced by the pointer NewP, must be inserted after the person referenced by Pt. See Figure 10.d.

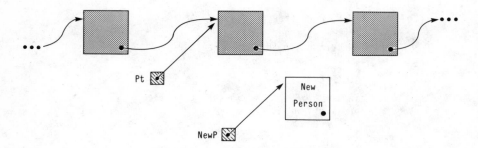

Figure 10.d   Linked List Before Insertion

Insertion is a simple matter of changing the pointers:

```
NewP↑.Next := Pt↑.Next;
Pt↑.Next := NewP
```

Figure 10.e illustrates the result.

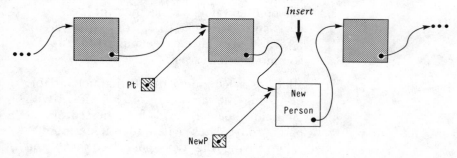

Figure 10.e   Linked List After Insertion

Deletion of the person following the auxiliary pointer Pt is accomplished in the single instruction:

```
Pt↑.Next := Pt↑.Next↑.Next
```

It is often practical to process a list using two pointers — a lookahead and a trailer, one following the other. In the case of deletion, it is then likely that one pointer — say P1 — precedes the member to be deleted, and P2 points to that member. Deletion can then be expressed in the single instruction:

```
P1↑.Next := P2↑.Next
```

You are, however, warned that deletions in this manner will sometimes result in the loss of usable (free) storage. A possible remedy is to maintain an explicit list of "deleted" members, pointed to by a variable Free. New variables will then be taken from this list (if it is not empty) instead of using the procedure New. A deletion of a list member now becomes a transfer of that member from the list to the free-member list.

```
P1↑.Next := P2↑.Next;
P2↑.Next := Free;
Free := P2
```

Finally, by using the predeclared procedure Dispose, the management of deleted members can be left to the Pascal implementation.

Dispose(Q)   deallocates the identified variable Q↑ and destroys the identifying value Q. It is an error if Q is nil or undefined. The value Q must have been created with the first form of New.

Dispose(Q,K1,...,Kn)   deallocates the identified variant record variable Q↑ with active variants selected by K1,...,Kn and destroys the identifying value Q. It is an error if Q is nil or undefined. The value Q must have been created with the second form of New and K1,...,Kn must select the same variants selected when Q was created.

Chapter 11 presents Programs 11.6 and 11.7 illustrating the traversal of tree structures which are constructed using pointer types.

CHAPTER 11

Procedures and Functions

As we grow in the art of computer programming, we construct programs in a sequence of *refinement steps*. At each step we break our task into a number of subtasks, thereby defining a number of partial programs. To camouflage this structure is undesirable. The concepts of the *procedure* and *function* allow you to display the subtasks as explicit subprograms.

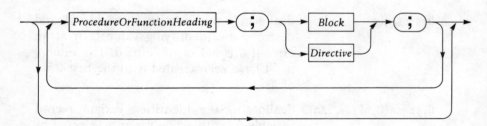

Figure 11.a. Syntax diagram for *ProcedureAndFunctionDeclarationPart*

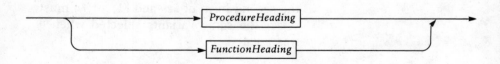

Figure 11.b. Syntax diagram for *ProcedureOrFunctionHeading*

11.A. Procedures

Throughout the example programs so far in this user manual, the predeclared procedures Read, Readln, Write, and Writeln are used. This section describes how to build your own "programmer-declared" procedures; in fact, Programs 8.2 and 10.1 use them.

The *procedure declaration* serves to define a program part and to associate it with an identifier, so that it can be activated by a *procedure statement*. The declaration has the same form as a program, except it is introduced by a *procedure heading* instead of a program heading.

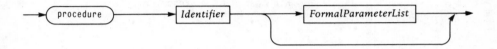

Figure 11.c. Syntax diagram for *ProcedureHeading*

Recall Program 6.1 that found the minimum and maximum values in a list of integers. As an extension, say that n increments are added to A[1]...A[n], then Min and Max are again computed. The resulting program, which employs a procedure to determine Min and Max, follows.

```
program MinMax2(Input,Output);

    { Program 11.1 - Extend Program 6.1 by introducing a procedure. }

    const
        MaxSize = 20;

    type
        ListSize = 1..MaxSize;

    var
        Increment: Integer;
        Item: ListSize;
        A: array [ListSize] of Integer;

    procedure MinMax;
        var
            Item: ListSize;
            Min, Max, First, Second: Integer;
```

```
      begin
         Min := A[1];   Max := Min;   Item := 2;
         while Item < MaxSize do
            begin  First := A[Item];   Second:= A[Item+1];
               if First > Second then
                  begin
                     if First > Max then Max := First;
                     if Second < Min then Min := Second
                  end
               else
                  begin
                     if Second > Max then Max := Second;
                     if First < Min then Min := First
                  end;
               Item := Item + 2
            end;
         if Item = MaxSize then
            if A[MaxSize] > Max then Max := A[MaxSize]
            else
               if A[MaxSize] < Min then Min := A[MaxSize];
         Writeln(Output, Max, Min);  Writeln(Output)
      end {MinMax};

begin
   for Item := 1 to MaxSize do
      begin  Read(Input, A[Item]);   Write(Output, A[Item] :4)  end;
   Writeln(Output);
   MinMax;
   for Item := 1 to MaxSize do
      begin
         Read(Input, Increment);   A[Item] := A[Item] + Increment;
         Write(Output, A[Item] :4)
      end;
   Writeln(Output);
   MinMax
end .
```

Produces as results:

```
 -1  -3   4   7   8  54  23  -5   3   9   9   9  -6  45  79  79   3   1   1   5

        79          -6


 44  40   7  15   9  88  15  -4   7  43  12  17  -7  48  59  39   9   7   7  12

        88          -7
```

Although simple, this program illustrates many points:

1. The simplest form of the *procedure heading*, namely:

   procedure *Identifier;*

2. *Blocks.* A procedure is a block with a name. The program block is MinMax2 and the procedure block is MinMax. In this case the part of the Program 6.1 used only to find the minimum and maximum values is isolated and given the name MinMax. Just like the program block, the block constituting a procedure has a declaration part which introduces the objects local to the procedure.

3. *Local Variables.* Local to procedure MinMax are the variables Item, First, Second, Min and Max; assignments to these variables have no effect on the program outside the scope of MinMax. Local variables are undefined at the beginning of the statement part each time the procedure is activated.

4. *Global Variables.* A, Item and Increment are global variables declared in the main program. They may be referenced throughout the program (e.g., the first assignment in MinMax is Min := A[1]).

5. *Scope.* Note that Item is the name for both a global and a local variable. These are not the same variable! A procedure may refer to any variable non-local to it, or it may choose to redefine the name. If a variable name is redeclared, the new name/type association is then valid for the scope of the defining procedure, and the global variable of that name (unless passed as a parameter) is no longer available within the procedure scope. Assignment to the local variable Item (e.g., Item := Item+2) has no effect upon the global variable Item, and because within MinMax the local Item has precedence, the global Item is effectively inaccessible.

   It is a good programming practice to declare every identifier which is not referred to outside the procedure, as strictly local to that procedure. Not only is this good documentation, but it also provides added security. For example, Item could have been left as a global variable; but then a later extension to the program which activated procedure MinMax within a loop controlled by Item would cause incorrect computation.

6. The *Procedure Statement.* In this example the statement MinMax in the main program activates the procedure.

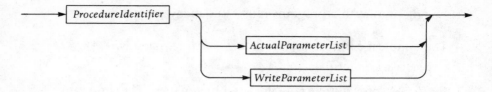

Figure 11.d.   Syntax diagram for *ProcedureStatement*

Examining Program 11.1 in more detail, note that MinMax is activated twice. By formulating the program part as a procedure − i.e., by not explicitly writing this program part twice − you can conserve not only your typing time, but also the memory (space) used by the program. The static code is stored only once, and the space for local variables is dynamically activated only during the execution of the procedure (created at the beginning and destroyed at the end).

You should not hesitate, however, from formulating an action as a procedure − even when called only once − if doing so enhances the readability of a program. In general, shorter blocks are easier to understand than long ones. Defining development steps as procedures makes a more communicable and verifiable program.

11.A.1   Parameter lists

Often necessary with the decomposition of a problem into subprograms is the introduction of new variables to represent the arguments and the results of the subprograms. The purpose of such variables should be clear from the program text.

Program 11.2 extends the above example to compute the minimum and maximum value of an array in a more general sense. This illustrates several further points about procedures.

1. The second form of the *procedure heading,* i.e., with a parameter list.

2. *Formal Parameters.* The *parameter list* gives the name of each formal parameter followed by its type. MinMax has L, Min, and Max as formal parameters. The formal parameter list opens a new scope for the parameters.

3. *Actual Parameters.* Note a correspondence between the procedure heading and the procedure statement. The latter contains a list of *actual parameters,* which are substituted for the

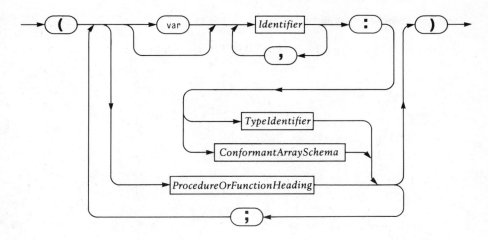

Figure 11.e. Syntax diagram for *FormalParameterList*

corresponding formal parameters that are defined in the procedure declaration. The correspondence is established by the positioning of the parameters in the lists of actual and formal parameters. Parameters provide a substitution mechanism that allows a process to be repeated with a variation of its arguments (e.g., MinMax is activated twice to scan array A and once to scan array B).

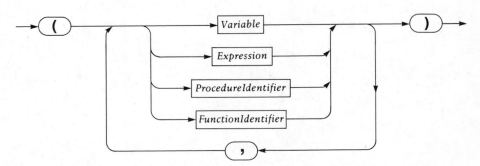

Figure 11.f. Syntax diagram for *ActualParameterList*

There exist four kinds of parameters: value parameters, variable parameters, procedural parameters (described in Section 11.A.4), and functional parameters (described in Section 11.B.1).

```
program MinMax3(Input,Output);

    { Program 11.2 - Modify Program 11.1 for two lists. }

    const
        MaxSize = 20;

    type
        ListSize = 1..MaxSize;
        List = array [ListSize] of Integer;

    var
        Item: ListSize;
        A, B: List;
        MinA, MinB, MaxA, MaxB: Integer;

    procedure MinMax(var L: List; var Min, Max: Integer);
        var
            Item: ListSize;
            First, Second: Integer;

    begin
        Min := L[1];  Max := Min;  Item := 2;
        while Item < MaxSize do
            begin  First := L[Item];  Second:= L[Item+1];
                if First > Second then
                    begin
                        if First > Max then Max := First;
                        if Second < Min then Min := Second
                    end
                else
                    begin
                        if Second > Max then Max := Second;
                        if First < Min then Min := First
                    end;
                Item := Item + 2
            end;
        if Item = MaxSize then
            if L[MaxSize] > Max then Max := L[MaxSize]
            else
                if L[MaxSize] < Min then Min := L[MaxSize]
    end { MinMax };
```

```
   procedure ReadWrite(var L: List);
   begin
      for Item := 1 to MaxSize do
         begin Read(Input, L[item]);  Write(Output, L[Item] :4)  end;
      Writeln(Output)
   end { ReadWrite };

begin { main program }
   ReadWrite(A);
   MinMax(A, MinA, MaxA);
   Writeln(Output, MinA, MaxA, MaxA - MinA);  Writeln(Output);
   ReadWrite(B);
   MinMax(B, MinB, MaxB);
   Writeln(Output, MinB, MaxB, MaxB - MinB);  Writeln(Output);
   Writeln(Output);
   Writeln(Output, abs(MinA - MinB), abs(MaxA - MaxB));
   Writeln(Output);
   for Item := 1 to MaxSize do
      begin
         A[Item] := A[Item] + B[Item];
         Write(Output, A[Item] :4)
      end;
   Writeln(Output);
   MinMax(A, MinA, MaxA);
   Writeln(Output, MinA, MaxA, MaxA - MinA)
end .
```

Produces as results:

```
-1  -3   4   7   8  54  23  -5   3   9   9   9  -6  45  79  79   3   1   1   5
        -6          79          85

45  43   3   8   1  34  -8   1   4  34   3   8  -1   3  -2  -4   6   6   6   7
        -8          45          53


         2          34

44  40   7  15   9  88  15  -4   7  43  12  17  -7  48  77  75   9   7   7  12
        -7          88          95
```

4. *Variable Parameters*. Procedure MinMax shows the case of the *variable parameter*. The actual parameter *must be a variable;* the corresponding formal parameter must be preceded by the symbol var and becomes a synonym for this actual variable during the entire execution of the procedure. Any operation involving the formal parameter is then performed directly upon the actual paramter. Use variable parameters to represent the *results* of a procedure — as is the case for Min and Max in Program 11.2. Furthermore, if X1..Xn are the actual variables that correspond to the formal variable parameters V1..Vn, then X1..Xn should be *distinct* variables. All address calculations are done at the time of the procedure activation. Hence, if a variable is a component of an array, its index expression is evaluated when the procedure is activated. Note that a component of a packed structure or a tag field in a variant record must not appear as an actual variable parameter, thus avoiding implementation problems for calculating addresses.

When no symbol heads the parameter section, the parameter(s) of this section are said to be *value parameter(s)*. In this case the actual parameter *must be an expression* (of which a variable is a simple case). The corresponding formal parameter represents a local variable in the activated procedure. As its initial value, this variable receives the current value of the corresponding actual parameter (i.e., the value of the expression at the time of the procedure activation). The procedure may then change the value of this variable through an assignment; this cannot, however, affect the value of the actual parameter. Hence, a value parameter can never represent a result of a computation. Note that file parameters or structured variables with files as components may not be specified as actual value parameters, as this would constitute an assignment.

The difference in the effects of value and variable parameters is shown in Program 11.3.

The table below summarizes the correct kinds of parameters for formal and actual parameter lists.

	formal parameter	**actual parameter**
value parameter	variable identifier	expression
variable parameter	variable identifier	variable
procedural parameter	procedure heading	procedure identifier
functional parameter	function heading	function identifier

```
program Parameters(Output);

   { Program 11.3 - Illustrate value and var parameters. }

   var
      A, B: Integer;

   procedure Add1(X: Integer; var Y: Integer);
   begin
      X := X + 1;  Y := Y + 1;  Writeln(Output,X,Y)
   end { Add1 };

begin
   A := 0;  B := 0;  Add1(A,B);
   Writeln(Output,A,B)
end { Parameters }.
```

Produces as results:

```
   1       1
   0       1
```

In procedure MinMax of Program 11.2 none of the values in array L are altered; i.e., L is not a result. Consequently L could have been defined as a value parameter without affecting the end result. To understand why this was not done, it is helpful to look at the implementation.

A procedure *activation* allocates a new area for each value parameter; this represents the local variable. The current value of the actual parameter is "copied" into this location; exit from the procedure simply releases this storage.

If a parameter is not used to transfer a result of the procedure, a value parameter is generally preferred. The accessing may be more efficient, and you are protected against mistakenly altering the data. However in the case where a parameter is of a structured type (e.g., an array), you should be cautious, for the copying operation is relatively expensive, and the amount of storage needed to hold the copy may be large. In the example, because each component in the array L is accessed only once, it is desirable to define the parameter as a variable parameter.

We may change the dimension of the array simply by redefining MaxSize. To make the program applicable for an array of reals, we need only change the type and variable definitions; the statements are not dependent upon integer data.

11.A.2.   Conformant-array parameters

Another way to pass different-sized arrays to a procedure or function is to use a conformant-array parameter as a variable or value parameter in the formal parameter list. Caution: Conformant array parameters are an optional feature in the ISO Pascal Standard. Some implementations will not support them.

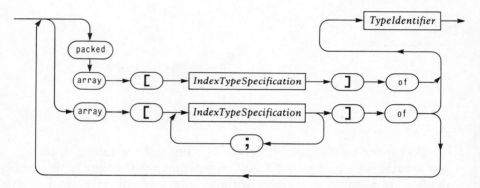

Figure 11.g.   Syntax diagram for *ConformantArraySchema*

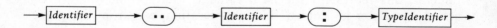

Figure 11.h.   Syntax diagram for *IndexTypeSpecification*

Conformant arrays specify the actual bounds of each dimension of the array as bound identifiers which are a kind of read-only variable. The index type of the actual array parameter must be compatible with the type in the conformant array's index type specification. The smallest and largest values of that index type must lie within the closed interval of the type in the index type specification. The component types must be the same, and if the component type of the conformant array parameter is another conformant array parameter then the component type of the actual array parameter must conform to it.

A conformant array parameter may be packed only in its last dimension. Actual parameters to value conformant array parameters may be variables or strings.

The MatrixMul program of Chapter 6 is rewritten as Program 11.4 to use conformant array parameters. Program 11.7 passes different-length strings to a formal conformant-array parameter.

11.A.3   Recursive procedures

The use of a procedure identifier within the text of the procedure itself implies *recursive* execution of the procedure. Problems whose definition is naturally recursive, often lend themselves to recursive solutions. An example is Program 11.5.

The task is to construct a program to convert expressions into postfix form (Polish notation). This is done by constructing an individual conversion procedure for each syntactic construct (expression, term, factor). As these syntactic constructs are defined recursively, their corresponding procedures may activate themselves recursively.

Given as data are the symbolic expressions:

```
(a+b)*(c-d)
a+b*c-d
(   a   * b)*   c-d
a+b*(c-d)
a*a*a*a
b+c*(d+c*a*a)*b+a  .
```

which are formed accordng to the EBNF below. A period terminates the input.

Expression = Term { ("+" | "−") Term } .

Term = Factor { "" Factor }.*

Factor = Identifier | "(" Expression ")" .

Identifier = Letter .

```
program MatrixMul2(Input, Output);

    { Program 11.4 - Rewrite Program 6.3 using a procedure with
                     conformant-array parameters. }

    const
        M = 4;  P = 3;  N = 2;

    type
        Positive = 1..MaxInt;

    var
        A: array [1..M, 1..P] of Integer;
        B: array [1..P, 1..N] of Integer;
        C: array [1..M, 1..N] of Integer;

    procedure ReadMatrix
        (var X: array [LoRow..HiRow: Positive;
                       LoCol..HiCol: Positive] of Integer);

        var
            Row, Col: Positive;
    begin
        for Row := 1 to HiRow do
            for Col := 1 to HiCol do
                Read(Input, X[Row,Col])
    end { ReadMatrix };

    procedure WriteMatrix
        (var X: array [LoRow..HiRow: Positive;
                       LoCol..HiCol: Positive] of Integer);
        var
            Row, Col: Positive;
    begin
        for Row := 1 to HiRow do
            begin
                for Col := 1 to HiCol do
                    Write(Output, X[Row,Col]);
                Writeln(Output)
            end
    end { WriteMatrix }

    procedure Multiply
        (var A: array [LoARow..HiARow: Positive;
                       LoACol..HiACol: Positive] of Integer;
         var B: array [LoBRow..HiBRow: Positive;
                       LoBCol..HiBCol: Positive] of Integer;
         var C: array [LoCRow..HiCRow: Positive;
                       LoCCol..HiCCol: Positive] of Integer);
```

```
      var
         Sum: Integer;
         I, J, K: Positive;
   begin
      if (LoARow <> 1) or (LoACol <> 1) or (LoBRow <> 1) or
         (LoBCol <> 1) or (LoCRow <> 1) or (LoCCol <> 1) or
         (HiARow <> HiCRow) or (HiACol <> HiBRow) or
         (HiBCol <> HiCCol) then {error}
      else
         for I := 1 to HiCRow do
            begin
               for J := 1 to HiCCol do
                  begin  Sum := 0;
                     for K := 1 to HiACol do
                        Sum := Sum + A[I,K] * B[K,J];
                     C[I,J] := Sum
                  end;
            end
   end { Multiply };

begin
   ReadMatrix(A);
   WriteMatrix(A);
   ReadMatrix(B);
   WriteMatrix(B);
   Multiply(A,B,C);
   WriteMatrix(C)
end .
```

Produces as results:

```
      1           2           3
     -2           0           2
      1           0           1
     -1           2          -3

     -1           3
     -2           2
      2           1

      1          10
      6          -4
      1           4
     -9          -2
```

```
program PostFix(Input,Output);

   { Program 11.5 - Convert an infix expression to Polish postfix form. }

   label 13 { premature end of file };

   var
      Ch: Char;

   procedure Find;
   begin
      if Eof(Input) then goto 13;
      repeat  Read(Input, Ch);
      until (Ch <> ' ') or Eof(Input)
   end { Find };

   procedure Expression;
      var
         Op: Char;

      procedure Term;

         procedure Factor;
         begin
            if Ch = '(' then
               begin  Find;  Expression;  { Ch = ')' }  end
            else
               Write(Output, Ch);
            Find
         end { Factor };

      begin { Term }
         Factor;
         while Ch = '*' do
            begin  Find;  Factor;  Write(Output, '*')
            end
      end { Term };

   begin { Expression }
      Term;
      while (Ch = '+') or (Ch = '-') do
         begin
            Op := Ch;  Find;  Term;  Write(Output, Op)
         end
   end { Expression };
```

```
begin { PostFix }
   Find;
   repeat
     Expression;
     Writeln(Output)
   until Ch = '.';
13:
end { PostFix } .
```

Produces as results:

```
ab+cd-*
abc*+d-
ab+c*d-
abcd-*+
aa*a*a*
bcdca*a*+*b*+a+
```

The *binary tree* is a data structure that is naturally defined in recursive terms and processed by recursive algorithms. It consists of a finite set of nodes that is either empty or else consists of a node (the root) with two disjoint binary trees, called the left and right subtrees [Reference 6]. Recursive procedures for generating and traversing binary trees naturally reflect this mode of definition.

Program 11.6 builds a binary tree and traverses it in pre-, in-, and postorder. The tree is specified in preorder, i.e., by listing the nodes (single letters in this case) starting at the root and following first the left and then the right subtrees so that the input corresponding to Figure 11.i is:

```
abc..de..fg...hi..jkl..m..n..
```

where a point signifies an empty subtree.

11.A.4   Procedural parameters

We can rewrite Program 11.6 to illustrate passing procedures as parameters. Procedural parameters appear in the formal parameter list of procedures and functions as procedure headings. In the corresponding actual parameter list only the procedure identifier must be specified. Program 11.7 illustrates this as well as the passing of actual string values to conformant array parameters.

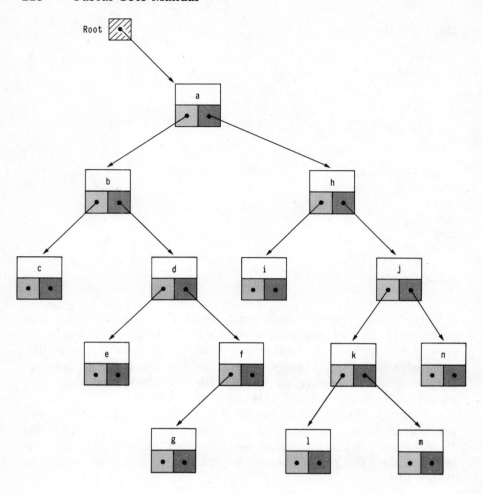

Figure 11.i.   Binary Tree Structure

```
program Traversal(Input,Output);

    { Program 11.6 - Illustrate binary tree traversal. }

    type
        Ptr = ↑Node;
        Node =
            record
                Info: Char;
                LLink, RLink: Ptr
            end;
```

```
var
   Root: Ptr;
   Ch: Char;
procedure PreOrder(P: Ptr);
begin
   if P <> nil then
      begin
         Write(Output,P↑.Info); PreOrder(P↑.LLink); PreOrder(P↑.RLink)
      end
end { PreOrder };
procedure InOrder(P: Ptr);
begin
   if P <> nil then
      begin
         InOrder(P↑.LLink); Write(Output, P↑.Info); InOrder(P↑.RLink)
      end
end { InOrder };
procedure PostOrder(P: Ptr);
begin
   if P <> nil then
      begin
         PostOrder(P↑.LLink);PostOrder(P↑.RLink);Write(Output,P↑.Info)
      end
end { PostOrder };
procedure Enter(var P: Ptr);
begin  Read(Input, Ch);  Write(Output, Ch);
   if Ch <> '.' then
      begin  New(P);
         P↑.Info := Ch; Enter(P↑.LLink); Enter(P↑.RLink)
      end
   else  P := nil
end { Enter };
begin { Traversal }
   Enter(Root);  Writeln(Output);
   PreOrder(Root);  Writeln(Output);
   InOrder(Root);  Writeln(Output);
   PostOrder(Root);  Writeln(Output)
end { Traversal } .
```

Produces as results:

```
abc..de..fg...hi..jkl..m..n..
abcdefghijklmn
cbedgfaihlkmjn
cegfdbilmknjha
```

```
program Traversal2(Input,Output);

  { Program 11.7 - Rewrite Program 11.6 using procedural parameters. }
  type
      Ptr = ↑Node;
      Node =
        record
            Info: Char;
            LLink, RLink: Ptr
        end;
      Positive = 1..MaxInt;

  var
      Root: Ptr;
      Ch: Char;

  procedure PreOrder(P: Ptr);
  begin
    if P <> nil then
      begin
          Write(Output,P↑.Info); PreOrder(P↑.LLink); PreOrder(P↑.RLink)
      end
  end { PreOrder };

  procedure InOrder(P: Ptr);
  begin
    if P <> nil then
      begin
          InOrder(P↑.LLink); Write(Output, P↑.Info); InOrder(P↑.RLink)
      end
  end { InOrder };

  procedure PostOrder(P: Ptr);
  begin
    if P <> nil then
      begin
          PostOrder(P↑.LLink); PostOrder(P↑.RLink); Write(Output,P↑.Info)
      end
  end { PostOrder };

  procedure Enter(var P: Ptr);
  begin  Read(Input, Ch); Write(Output, Ch);
    if Ch <> '.' then
      begin  New(P);
          P↑.Info := Ch; Enter(P↑.LLink); Enter(P↑.RLink)
      end
    else  P := nil
  end { Enter };
```

```
procedure WriteNodes(procedure TreeOperation(Start: Ptr); Root: Ptr;
                Title: packed array [M..N: Positive] of Char);
    var
        C: Positive;
    begin
        Writeln(Output);
        for C := M to N do Write(Output, Title[C]);
        Writeln(Output); Writeln(Output);
        TreeOperation(Root); Writeln(Output)
    end { WriteNodes };
begin { Traversal2 }
    Enter(Root); Writeln(Output);
    WriteNodes(PreOrder, Root, 'Nodes listed in preorder:');
    WriteNodes(InOrder, Root, 'Nodes listed inorder:');
    WriteNodes(PostOrder, Root, 'Nodes listed in postorder:')
end { Traversal2 } .
```

Produces as results:

```
abc..de..fg...hi..jkl..m..n..

Nodes listed in preorder:

abcdefghijklmn

Nodes listed inorder:

cbedgfaihlkmjn

Nodes listed in postorder:

cegfdbilmknjha
```

Be careful of applying recursive techniques indiscriminately. Although appearing "clever," they do not always produce the most computationally efficient solutions.

If a procedure P activates a procedure Q and Q also activates P, and neither is declared within the other, then either P or Q must be declared by a *forward declaration* (Section 11.C).

The predeclared *procedures* in Appendix A are provided in every implementation of Standard Pascal. Any implementation may feature additional predeclared procedures. Since they are, as all predeclared and predefined objects, assumed to have a scope surrounding the user program, no conflict arises from a declaration redefining the same identifier within the program.

Predeclared procedures may not be passed as actual procedural parameters.

11.B.   Functions

Functions are program parts (in the same sense as procedures) which compute a single ordinal, real, or pointer value for use in the evaluation of an expression. A *function designator* specifies the activation of a function and consists of the identifier denoting the function and a list of actual parameters. The parameters are variables, expressions, procedures, or functions and are substituted for the corresponding formal parameters.

The function declaration has the same form as the program, with the exception of the *function heading* which has the form:

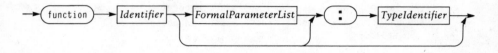

Figure 11.j.   Syntax diagram for *FunctionHeading*

As in the case of procedures, the labels in the label declaration part and all identifiers introduced in the the constant definition part, the type definition part, the variable, procedure, or function declaration parts are *local* to the function declaration, which is called the *scope* of these objects. They are not known outside their scope. The values of local variables are undefined at the beginning of the statement part.

The identifier specified in the function heading names the function. The result type must be a simple or pointer type. Within the function declaration there must be an executed assignment (of the result type) to the function identifier. This assignment "returns" the result of the function.

Program 11.8 formulates the exponentiation algorithm of Program 4.3 as a function declaration.

The appearance of the function identifier in an expression within the function itself implies *resursive* execution of the function. The first example in Appendix F illustrates a recursive function.

Function designators may occur before the function declaration if there is a *forward declaration* (Section 11.C).

The predeclared *functions* of Appendix A are assumed to be provided in every implementation of Standard Pascal. Any implementation may feature additional predeclared functions. Predeclared functions may not be passed as actual functional parameters.

```
program Exponentiation2(Output);

    { Program 11.8 - Reformulate Program 4.6 using a function. }

    type
        Natural = 0..MaxInt;

    var
        Pi, PiSquared: Real;

    function Power(Base: Real; Exponent: Natural): Real;
        var
            Result: Real;
    begin  Result := 1;
        while Exponent > 0 do
            begin
                while not Odd(Exponent) do
                    begin  Exponent := Exponent div 2; Base := Sqr(Base)
                    end;
                Exponent := Exponent - 1; Result := Result * Base
            end;
        Power := Result
    end { Power };

begin  Pi := ArcTan(1.0) * 4;
    Writeln(Output, 2.0 :11:6, 7 :3, Power(2.0,7) :11:6);
    PiSquared := Power(Pi,2);
    Writeln(Output, Pi  :11:6, 2 :3, PiSquared     :11:6);
    Writeln(Output, PiSquared :11:6, 2 :3, Power(PiSquared, 2) :11:6);
    Writeln(Output, Pi  :11:6, 4 :3, Power(Pi,4)   :11:6)
end { Exponentiation2 } .
```

Produces as results:

```
2.000000  7 128.000000
3.141593  2   9.869605
9.869605  2  97.409100
3.141593  4  97.409100
```

11.B.1   Functional parameters

Functions themselves may also be passed as parameters to procedures and functions. A formal functional parameter is specified by a function heading; its corresponding actual parameter is a function identifier. Program 11.9 computes the sum of terms in a series for different functions specified at the time of the call.

```pascal
program SumSeries(Output);

   { Program 11.9 - Write a table of a series sum progression. }

   const
      MaxTerms = 10;

   var
      Term: 1..MaxTerms;

   function Sigma(function F(X:Real):Real;Lower,Upper:Integer):Real;
      var
         Index: Integer;
         Sum: Real;
   begin
      Sum := 0.0;
      for Index := Lower to Upper do
         Sum := Sum + F(Index);
      Sigma := Sum
   end { Sigma };

   function IncreasingSine(X: Real): Real;
   begin
      IncreasingSine := sin(X) * X
   end { IncreasingSine };

   function InverseCube(X: Real): Real;
   begin
      InverseCube := 1 / (Sqr(X) * X)
   end { InverseCube };

begin { SumSeries }
   for Term := 1 to MaxTerms do
     Writeln(Term,Sigma(IncreasingSine,1,Term), Sigma(InverseCube,1,Term))
end { SumSeries } .
```

Produces as results:

```
 1 8.414710E-01 1.000000E+00
 2 2.660066E+00 1.125000E+00
 3 3.083426E+00 1.162037E+00
 4 5.621672E-02 1.177662E+00
 5-4.738405E+00 1.185662E+00
 6-6.414900E+00 1.190292E+00
 7-1.815995E+00 1.193207E+00
 8 6.098872E+00 1.195160E+00
 9 9.807942E+00 1.196532E+00
10 4.367733E+00 1.197532E+00
```

11.B.2 Side Effects

An assignment (occurring in a function declaration) to a non-local variable or to a variable parameter is called a *side effect*. Such occurrences often disguise the intent of the program and greatly complicate the task of verification. Hence, the use of functions producing side effects is strongly discouraged. As an example, consider Program 11.10.

11.C. Forward Declarations

Procedure (function) identifiers may be used before the procedure (function) declaration if there is a *forward declaration*. Forward declarations are necessary to allow mutually recursive procedures and functions that are not nested. The form is as follows: (Notice that the parameter list and result type are written *only* in the forward reference.)

```
procedure Q(X: T); Forward;

procedure P(Y: T);
begin
   Q(A)
end;

procedure Q; { parameters and result types are not repeated }
begin
   P(B)
end;
```

```
program SideEffect(Output);

   { Program 11.10 - Illustrate function side effects. }

   var
      A, Z: Integer;

   function Sneaky(X: Integer): Integer;
   begin
      Z := Z - X { side effect on Z };
      Sneaky := Sqr(X)
   end { Sneaky };

begin
   Z := 10;   A := Sneaky(Z);
   Writeln(Output, A, Z);
   Z := 10;   A := Sneaky(10);   A := A * Sneaky(Z);
   Writeln(Output, A, Z);
   Z := 10;   A := Sneaky(Z);   A := A * Sneaky(10);
   Writeln(Output, A, Z);
end { SideEffect } .
```

Produces as results:

```
      100          0
        0          0
    10000        -10
```

CHAPTER 12

Textfile Input and Output

Communication between people and computer systems was already mentioned in Chapter 9, File Types. Both learn to *understand* through what is termed *pattern recognition*. Unfortunately, the patterns recognized most easily by people (mainly those of picture and sound) are very different from those acceptable to computer systems (electrical impulses). In fact, the expense of physically transmitting data — implying a translation of patterns legible to people into those legible to computer systems and vice versa — can be as costly as the processing of the data itself. (Consequently, much research is devoted to minimizing the cost by "automating" more of the translation process.) This task of communication is called input and output handling (I/O).

People can transmit information to computer systems via *input devices* and *media* (e.g., keyboards, diskettes, pointing devices, tape cartridges, magnetic tapes, terminals) and receive results via *output devices* and *media* (e.g., line printers, magnetic tapes, diskettes, tape cartridges, plotters, speakers, and video displays). What is common to most of these — and defined by each individual computer installation — is a set of legible characters (Chapter 2). It is over this character set that Pascal defines the standard type Text (see Chapter 9).

It is important to remember that each such input-output device enforces certain conventions as to the meaning of specific characters and patterns (strings) of characters. For example, most printers enforce some maximum line length. Also, many older line printers interpret the first character of each line as a "carriage control" character, which is not printed but may cause some action such as a page eject or overprinting. When a textfile is used to represent a particular device, the program must obey the conventions for using that device.

Textfiles may be accessed through the predeclared file procedures Get and Put. This can, of course, be quite cumbersome as these procedures are defined for single-character manipulation. To illustrate, suppose we have a natural number stored in a variable X and wish to write it on the file output. Note that the pattern of characters denoting the decimal representation of the value will be quite different from that denoting the value written as a Roman numeral (see Program 4.9). But as we are usually interested in decimal notation, it appears sensible to offer built-in, standard, transformation procedures that translate abstract numbers (from whatever computer-internal representation is used) into sequences of decimal digits and vice versa.

The two predeclared procedures Read and Write are thereby extended in several ways to facilitate the analysis and the formation of textfiles.

12.A.   The Standard Files Input and Output

The standard textfiles Input and Output usually represent the standard I/O media of a computer system (such as the keyboard and the video display). Hence, they are the principal communication line between the computer system and its human user.

Because these two files are used very frequently, they are considered as "default values" in textfile operations when the textfile F is not explicitly indicated. That is

```
Write(Ch)   =   Write(Output,Ch)
Read(Ch)    =   Read(Input,Ch)
Writeln     =   Writeln(Output)
Readln      =   Readln(Input)
Eof         =   Eof(Input)
Eoln        =   Eoln(Input)
Page        =   Page(Output) (See Section 12.D.)
```

If any of these procedures and functions are used without indication of a file parameter, the default convention specifies that the file Input or Output is assumed; in which case, it *must* be placed in the parameter list of the program heading.

Note: The effect of applying the predeclared procedure Reset or Rewrite to either Input or Output is implementation-defined.

Accordingly, reading and writing a textfile can be expressed as follows (assume var Ch: Char; B1, B2: Boolean; and P, Q, and R user-defined procedures).

Writing characters on file Output:

```
repeat
    repeat P(Ch); Write(Ch)
    until B1;
    Writeln
until B2
```

Reading characters from file Input:

```
while not eof do
    begin {process a line} P;
        while not eoln do
            begin Read(Ch); Q(Ch)
            end;
        R; Readln
    end
```

The next two examples of programs show the use of the textfiles Input and Output. (Consider what changes would be necessary if only Get and Put, not Read and Write, were to be used.)

```
program LetterFrequencies(Input,Output);

    { Program 12.1 - Perform a frequency count of letters in the
                     Input file; echo the input. }

    type
        Natural = 0..MaxInt;

    var
        Ch: Char;
        Count: array [Char] of Natural;
        Letters, Upper, Lower: set of Char;

    begin
        Upper := ['A','B','C','D','E','F','G','H','I','J','K','L','M',
                  'N','O','P','Q','R','S','T','U','V','W','X','Y','Z'];
```

```
  Lower := ['a','b','c','d','e','f','g','h','i','j','k','l','m',
            'n','o','p','q','r','s','t','u','v','w','x','y','z'];
  Letters := Lower + Upper;
  for Ch := 'A' to 'Z' do
     Count[Ch] := 0;
  for Ch := 'a' to 'z' do
     Count[Ch] := 0;
  while not Eof do
     begin
        while not Eoln do
           begin  Read(Ch);   Write(Ch);
              if Ch in Letters then Count[Ch] := Count[Ch] + 1
           end;
        Readln;   Writeln
     end;
  for Ch := 'A' to 'Z' do
     if Ch in Upper then Writeln(Ch, Count[Ch]);
  for Ch := 'a' to 'z' do
     if Ch in Lower then Writeln(Ch, Count[Ch]);
end .
```

Produces as results:

```
A rat in Tom's house might eat Tom's ice cream! (Arithmetic)
Pack my box with five dozen liquor jugs.
The quick brown fox jumped over the lazy sleeping dog.
A          2
B          0
C          0
D          0
E          0
F          0
G          0
H          0
I          0
J          0
K          0
L          0
M          0
N          0
```

O	0
P	1
Q	0
R	0
S	0
T	3
U	0
V	0
W	0
X	0
Y	0
Z	0
a	5
b	2
c	5
d	3
e	13
f	2
g	4
h	6
i	10
j	2
k	2
l	3
m	7
n	4
o	10
p	2
q	2
r	6
s	5
t	7
u	5
v	2
w	2
x	2
y	2
z	2

The following program copies Input to Output, inserting line numbers at the beginning of each line.

```pascal
program Addln(Input,Output);

    { Program 12.2 - Add line numbers to text file. }

    type
        Natural = 0..MaxInt;

    var
        LineNum: Natural;

begin
    LineNum := 0;
    while not Eof do
        begin
            LineNum := LineNum + 1;
            Write(LineNum :4, ' ');
            while not Eoln do
                begin
                    Write(Input↑);  Get(Input)
                end;
            Readln;  Writeln
        end
end .
```

Produces as results:

```
1 A rat in Tom's house might eat Tom's ice cream! (Arithmetic)
2 Pack my box with five dozen liquor jugs.
3 The quick brown fox jumped over the lazy sleeping dog.
```

When the file variable Input represents an input device (such as a keyboard) attached to an interactive terminal, most Pascal implementations delay evaluation of the buffer variable Input↑ until its value is actually required in the program. The use of Input↑ in expressions or implicitly as part of the action of Read, Readln, eof, or eoln causes its evaluation. Although an implicit Reset(Input) is done at the beginning of the program, the program will not wait for data from the terminal until it is needed — for example, when Input↑ is used. If the program writes a message to prompt its user for a response to be read in, the request for input will occur after the prompt has been written (just as you would expect ordinarily).

The program fragment below illustrates prompting a user at an interactive terminal:

```
program PromptExample(Input,Output);
    var Guess: Integer;
        .
        .
begin { Implicit Reset(Input) occurs here. }
    Writeln('Please enter an integer between 1 and 10.');
    Read(Guess)
        .
        .
```

A Pascal implementation *not* employing the delayed evaluation of Input↑ will cause a request or wait for data before the message is written because of the implicit Reset(Input) which occurs as the program begins executing. Whether or not delayed evaluation is supported is implementation-defined.

12.B. The Procedures Read and Readln

The procedure Read was defined for textfiles in Section 9.B. Read is extended not only to accept a variable number of parameters, but also to accept parameters of type Integer (or a subrange of Integer) and Real.

Let V1,V2,...,Vn denote variables of type Char, Integer, (or subrange of either) or Real, and let F denote a textfile.

Read(F,V) is an error if F is undefined or F is not in inspection mode or eof(F) is true.

1. Read(V1,...,Vn)   stands for
        Read(Input,V1,...,Vn)

2. Read(F,V1,...,Vn)   stands for
        begin Read(F,V1);...;Read(F,Vn) end

3. Readln(V1,...,Vn)   stands for
        Readln(Input,V1,...,Vn)

4. Readln(F,V1,...,Vn)   stands for
        begin Read(F,V1);...;Read(F,Vn); Readln(F) end

The effect for Readln is that after Vn is read (from the textfile F), the remainder of the current line is skipped. (However, the values of V1...Vn may stretch over several lines.)

5.   If Ch is a variable of type Char or subrange of Char, then

```
Read(F,Ch)     stands for
begin   Ch := F↑; Get(F)   end
```

6.   If a parameter V is of type Integer or a subrange Integer then Read accepts a sequence of characters forming a signed integer with possible leading blanks. The integer value denoted by this sequence is then assigned to V.

7.   If a parameter V is of type Real, Read accepts a sequence of characters forming a signed number with possible leading blanks. The real value denoted by this sequence is then assigned to V.

In scanning F (skipping blanks) to read numbers, Read may also skip end-of-line markers. F is left positioned to the non-digit character following the last digit constituting the number. To correctly read consecutive numbers, separate them by blanks or put them on separate lines. Read accepts the longest sequence of digits, and if two numbers are not separated, Read cannot distinguish them as two numbers (and neither can people!).

Examples:

Read and process a sequence of numbers where the last value is immediately followed by an asterisk. Assume F to be a textfile, X and Ch to be variables of types Integer (or Real) and Char respectively.

```
Reset(F);
repeat
   Read(F,X,Ch);
   P(X)
until Ch='*'
```

Perhaps a more common situation is when there is no way of knowing how many data items are to be read, and there is no special symbol that terminates the list. Two convenient schemata are show below. They make use of procedure SkipBlanks:

```
procedure SkipBlanks(var F: Text);
   var Done: Boolean;
begin
   Done := False;
   repeat
      if eof(F) then Done := True
      else
         if F↑ = ' ' then Get(F)
         else Done := True
   until Done
end
```

The first schema processes single numbers:

```
Reset(F);
while not eof(F) do
   begin
      Read(F,X); SkipBlanks(F);
      P(X);
   end
```

The second schema processes n-tuples of numbers:

```
Reset(F);
while not eof(F) do
   begin
      Read(F,X1,...,Xn); SkipBlanks(F)
      P(X1,...,Xn);
   end
```

For the above schema to function properly, the total number of single numbers must be a multiple of n.

12.C.   The Procedures Write and Writeln

The procedure Write was defined for textfiles in Section 9.B. Write is extended to accept a variable number of parameters whose types are compatible with Integer, Real, Boolean, or string types.

The procedure Write appends character strings (one or more characters) to a textfile. Let P1,P2, ... ,Pn be parameters of the form defined in the syntax diagram for *WriteParameterList* (Figure 12.a), and let F be a textfile. Then Write(F,P) is an error if F is undefined or F is not in generation mode or if eof(F) is not true.

1. `Write(P1,...,Pn)`   stands for
       `Write(Output,P1,...,Pn)`

2. `Write(F,P1,...,Pn)`   stands for
       `begin Write(F,P1);...,Write(F,Pn) end`

3. `Writeln(P1,...,Pn)`   stands for
       `Writeln(Output,P1,...,Pn)`

4. `Writeln(F,P1,...,Pn)`   stands for
       `begin Write(F,P1);...;Write(F,Pn); Writeln(F) end`

    `Writeln` has the effect of writing `P1,...,Pn` and then terminating the current line of the textfile F.

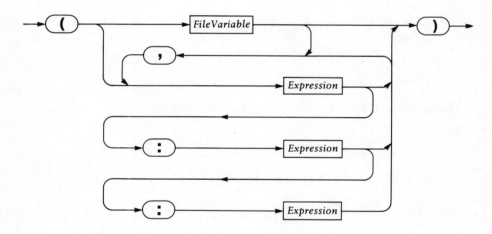

Figure 12.a.   Syntax diagram for *WriteParameterList*

5. Every parameter `Pi` must be of one of the forms:

       `e`
       `e: w`
       `e: w: f`

    where `e`, `w`, and `f` are expressions. `e` is the value to be written whose type is `Char`, `Integer`, any string, `Boolean`, or `Real`. `w` — called the minimum *field width* — is an optional control. `w` must be a positive integer expression and indicates the number of characters to be written. In general, `e` is written with `w` characters (with preceding blanks if necessary).

If no field width is specified, a default value is assumed according to the type of e. f — called the *fraction length* — is an optional control and is applicable only when e is of type Real. It must be a positive integer expression.

6. In the case where e has type Char, the default value of w is 1. Therefore Write(F,C) stands for f↑ := C; Put(F).

7. If e has type Integer, then default value of w is implementation defined. If w is less than the number of characters needed to write the integer, the entire representation of the integer (including a "–" if e is negative) is written anyway!

8. If e has a string type, the default value of w is the length of the string. If w is less than this length, then only the first w characters of e are written.

9. If e has type Boolean, the default value of w is implementation defined. One of the strings 'true' or 'false' is written according to 8. above depending on the value of w. Whether upper-case or lower-case (or even mixed-case) letters are written to represent the values true or false is implementation defined.

10. If e has type Real, the default value of w is implementation defined. If w is less than the number of characters needed to write the real number, more space is taken (including room for a "–" if e is negative). If f (the fraction length) is specified, the value of e will be written in *fixed-point* notation. Otherwise the value is written in decimal *floating-point* form using exponent notation.

    The general form for fixed-point notation is the sequence of characters: an optional minus sign (if the number is negative), a digit sequence representing the integer part, a period (decimal point), and a digit sequence representing the fraction part. The length of the fraction part is specified by f.

    The general form for floating-point form is the sequence of w characters: a blank or minus sign, one digit, a period (decimal point), a digit sequence, the letter E (or e), a plus sign or minus sign, and a digit sequence having an implementation-defined length representing the exponent. The length of the first digit sequence (preceding the letter E)

Char :   w   Write('$':w)

1    $

3         $

Integer   w   Write(-1984:w)   Write(1984:w)

1   - 1 9 8 4   1 9 8 4

4   - 1 9 8 4   1 9 8 4

5   - 1 9 8 4   1 9 8 4

7   - 1 9 8 4   1 9 8 4

strings   w   Write('hello':w)

1   h

3   h e l

5   h e l l o

7   h e l l o

Boolean   w   Write(false:w)   Write(true:w)

1   f   t

3   f a l   t r u

5   f a l s e   t r u e

7   f a l s e   t r u e

Figure 12.b.   Formatted Write Examples

Real	w	f	Write(123.789:w:f)	Write(-123.789:w:f)
	1	1	1 2 3 . 8	- 1 2 3 . 8
	1	3	1 2 3 . 7 8 9	- 1 2 3 . 7 8 9
	1	4	1 2 3 . 7 8 9 0	- 1 2 3 . 7 8 9 0
	5	1	1 2 3 . 8	- 1 2 3 . 8
	6	1	1 2 3 . 8	- 1 2 3 . 8
	7	1	1 2 3 . 8	- 1 2 3 . 8

w	Write(987.6:w)	Write(-987.6:w)
1	9 . 9 E + 0 2	- 9 . 9 E + 0 2
8	9 . 9 E + 0 2	- 9 . 9 E + 0 2
9	9 . 8 8 E + 0 2	- 9 . 8 8 E + 0 2
10	9 . 8 7 6 E + 0 2	- 9 . 8 7 6 E + 0 2
11	9 . 8 7 6 0 E + 0 2	- 9 . 8 7 6 0 E + 0 2

Figure 12.b.   Continued

will vary depending on the value of w. No additional preceding blanks are written for decimal floating-point form.

Figure 12.b gives examples of formatted writes with each type.

12.D.   The Procedure Page

As a convenience for formatting textfiles, Pascal has a predefined Page procedure. Page(F) is intended to cause subsequent text written on F to appear on a new "page" (if F is printed or displayed, etc.).

Page(F) causes an implementation-defined action on the file F. In most implementations, Page(F) writes the appropriate control characters (such as an ASCII Form Feed) to cause the desired effect.

Notes: If Page(F) is invoked and the last operation on F was not Writeln(F) then Page(F) performs an implicit Writeln(F) as its first action. F must be defined and in generation mode or else Page(F) is an error. The effect of reading a file F to which Page(F) has been applied is implementation-dependent.

REPORT

1. Introduction

The development of the language *Pascal* is based on two principal aims. The first is to make available a language suitable to teach programming as a systematic discipline based on certain fundamental concepts clearly and naturally reflected by the language. The second is to develop implementations of this language that are both reliable and efficient on presently available computers.

The desire for a new language for the purpose of teaching programming is due to my dissatisfaction with the presently used major languages whose features and constructs too often cannot be explained logically and convincingly and that too often defy systematic reasoning. Along with this dissatisfaction goes my conviction that the language in which students are taught to express their ideas profoundly influences their habits of thought and invention, and that the disorder governing these languages directly imposes itself onto the programming style of the students.

There is of course plenty of reason to be cautious with the introduction of yet another programming language, and the objection against teaching programming in a language which is not widely used and accepted has undoubtedly some justification, at least based on short-term commercial reasoning. However, the choice of a language for teaching based on its widespread acceptance and availability, together with the fact that the language most widely taught is therefore going to be the one most widely used, forms the safest recipe for stagnation in a subject of such profound pedagogical influence. I consider it therefore well worthwhile to make an effort to break this vicious circle.

Of course a new language should not be developed just for the sake of novelty; existing languages should be used as a basis for development wherever they meet the criteria mentioned and do not impede a systematic structure. In that sense Algol 60 was used as a basis for Pascal, since it meets the demands with respect to teaching to a much higher degree than any other standard language. Thus the principles of structuring, and in fact the form of expressions, are copied from Algol 60. It was, however, not deemed appropriate to adopt Algol 60 as a subset of Pascal; certain construction principles, particularly those of declarations, would have been incompatible with those allowing a natural and convenient representation of the additional features of Pascal.

The main extensions relative to Algol 60 lie in the domain of data-structuring facilities, since their lack in Algol 60 was considered as the prime cause for its relatively narrow range of applicability. The introduction of record and file structures should make it possible to solve commercial-type problems with Pascal, or at least to employ it successfully to demonstrate such problems in a programming course.

2. Summary of the Language

A computer program consists of two essential parts, a description of *actions* which are to be performed, and a description of the *data* that are manipulated by these actions. Actions are described by so-called *statements*, and data are described by so-called *declarations* and *definitions*.

The data are represented by values of *variables*. Every variable occurring in a statement must be introduced by a *variable declaration*, which associates an identifier and a data type with that variable. The *type* essentially defines the set of values that may be assumed by that variable, and restricts the set of valid operations on those values. A type in Pascal may be either directly described in the variable declaration, or it may be associated with a type identifier by a *type definition* and then represented by name.

The *simple* types are the predefined type Real and the various *ordinal* types. Every simple type defines an ordered set of values. Each ordinal type is characterized by a one-to-one mapping from its values to an interval of the integers — the so-called ordinal numbers of those values.

The basic ordinal types are the programmer-defined *enumerated* types and the predefined types Boolean, Char, and Integer. An enumerated type introduces a new set of values and a distinct identifier to denote each value. The values of Char are denoted by quotations, and the values of Integer and Real are denoted by numbers; these are syntactically distinct from identifiers. The set of values of type Char and their graphic representation vary from implementation to implementation, depending on the character set of each particular computer system.

Another ordinal type that may be defined is a *subrange* of any basic ordinal type (the host type) by indicating the smallest and largest values in the interval of values represented by the subrange.

The *structured* types are defined by describing the types of their components and by indicating a structuring method. The various structuring methods differ in the mechanism serving to access the components of a variable of the structured type. In Pascal, there are four basic structuring methods available: array structure, record structure, set structure, and file structure.

In an *array* structure, all components are of the same type. A component is accessed by a computable *index*, whose type is indicated in the array type description and which must be ordinal. It is usually an enumerated type or a subrange of Integer. Given a value of the index type, an *indexed variable* accesses one component of the array. Each array variable can therefore be regarded as a mapping of the index type onto the component type. The time needed for a component access does not depend on the value of the index. The array structure is therefore called a *random-access* structure.

In a *record* structure, the components (called *fields*) are not necessarily of the same type. In order that the type of a field be evident from the program text (without executing the program), a field is not specified by a computable value, but instead is specified by a unique identifier. These field identifiers are declared in the record type description. Again, the time needed to access any component does not depend on the field identifier, and the record is therefore also a random-access structure.

A record type may be specified as having several *variants*. This implies that different variables, although said to be of the same type, may assume structures that differ in a certain manner. The difference may consist of a different number and different types of components. The variant that is assumed by the current value of a record variable may be indicated by a component field which is common to all variants and is called the *tag field*. Usually, the part common to all variants will consist of several components, including the tag field.

A *set* structure defines the set of values that is the powerset of its base type, i.e., the set of all subsets of values of the base type. The base type must be an ordinal type, and will usually be an enumerated type, Char, or a subrange of Integer. Components (members) of sets are not directly accessed, but the set operations (including the membership operator) and a set-value *constructor* allow creation and manipulation of entire sets.

A *file* structure describes a *sequence* of components of the same type. A natural ordering of the components is defined through the sequence. At any instance, only one component is directly accessible, and it may be either inspected or generated but not both. The other components are accessed by progressing sequentially through the file. A file is generated by sequentially appending components at its end. Consequently, the file type description does not determine the number of components.

A variable declaration associates an identifier with a type, and when the block (see below) in which the declaration occurs is activated, a variable that is named by the identifier is created. Such variables that are declared in explicit declarations are sometimes called *static*. In contrast, variables may be generated by executable statement; such a *dynamic* generation yields a so-called *pointer* (a substitute for an explicit identifier) which subsequently serves to identify the variable. This pointer value may be assigned to variables and functions that possess its type. Each pointer type has a fixed *domain* type, and every variable identified by a pointer value of the pointer type possesses the domain type. In addition to such *identifying* values, each pointer type also has the value *nil* which points to no variable. Because components of structured variables may possess pointer types, and the domain type of pointer types may be structured, the use of pointers permits the representation of finite graphs in full generality.

The most fundamental statement is the *assignment* statement. It specifies that a value obtained by evaluating an *expression* be assigned to a variable (or component thereof). Expressions consist of variables, constants, array-parameter index bounds, set constructors, and operators and functions operating on the denoted quantities yielding result values. Variables, constants, and functions are either declared in the program or are standard ("predeclared") entities. Pascal defines a fixed set of operators, each of which can be regarded as describing a mapping from the operand types into the result type. The set of operators is divided into four groups.

1. *Arithmetic* operators are addition, subtraction, sign inversion, multiplication, division, and modulus.

2. *Boolean* operators are negation, union (or), and conjunction (and).

3. *Set* operators are union, intersection, and set difference.

4. *Relational* operators are equality, inequality, ordering, set membership, and set inclusion. The result type of relational operators is Boolean.

The *procedure* statement causes the execution of the designated procedure (see below). Assignment and procedure statements are the components, or "building blocks," of *structured* statements, which specify sequential, selective, or repeated execution of their components. Sequential execution of statements is specified by the *compound* statement, conditional or selective execution by the *if* and *case* statements, and repeated execution by the *repeat, while,* and *for* statements. The if statement serves to make the execution of a statement dependent on the value of a Boolean expression, and the case statement allows the selection among many statements according to the value of an ordinal expression. The for statement is used to execute the component statement when each of a succession of ordinal values is assigned to a so-called control variable. The repeat and while statements are used otherwise.

In addition, Pascal provides a *goto* statement, which indicates that execution is to continue at another place in the program; that place is marked by a *label*, which must be declared.

Statements and declarations of labels, constants, types, variables, procedures, and functions are collected together into *blocks*. The labels, constants, variables, types, procedures and functions declared in a block may be referred to only within that block, and therefore are called *local* to the block. Their identifiers have significance only within the program text that constitutes the block and that is called the *scope* of these identifiers. Blocks are the basis for declaring *programs, procedures,* and *functions*, in which a block is given a name (identifier) by which the block may be denoted. Since procedures and functions may be nested, scopes may be nested.

A procedure or function has a fixed number of parameters, each of which is denoted within the procedure or function by an identifier called the *formal* parameter. When a procedure or function is activated, an actual quantity has to be indicated for each parameter; the quantity can be referenced from inside the block of the procedure or function through the formal parameter. This quantity is called the *actual* parameter. There are four kinds of parameters: value parameters, variable parameters, procedural parameters, and functional parameters. In the first case, the actual parameter is an expression which is evaluated, and the value assigned to the formal parameter, once at the beginning of each activation of the procedure or function. The formal parameter represents a local variable. In the case of a variable parameter, the actual parameter denotes a variable and the formal parameter denotes the same variable during the entire activation of the procedure or function. In the case of procedural or functional parameters, the actual parameter is a procedure or function identifier.

A function is declared analogously to a procedure, except that the function yields a result which must possess the type that is specified in the function declaration. The result type is confined to be a simple type or a pointer type. Functions may be used as constituent in expressions. Assignments to non-local variables and other so-called side effects should be avoided within function declarations.

3.   Notation and Terminology

Syntactic constructs are denoted by descriptive English words (meta-identifiers) written in italics and are defined by rules in Extended Backus-Naur Form (EBNF) [Reference 13]. Each rule defines a meta-identifier by means of an EBNF expression, which consists of one or more alternative phrases separated by vertical bars (|). A phrase consists of zero or more elements, each of which is a meta-identifier, a literal symbol enclosed in quotes (" "), or another EBNF expression enclosed in matching braces, brackets, or parentheses. Braces { and } indicate repetition (zero or more occurrences), brackets [and] indicate optionality (zero or one occurrences), and parentheses (and) indicate grouping (exactly one occurrence) of the enclosed expression.

Within Section 4, EBNF rules describe the formation of lexical *symbols* from characters; additional characters must not occur within a symbol. Sections 5 through 13 use EBNF rules to define the syntax of programs in terms of symbols; symbols may be separated by (or preceded by) symbol *separators* as described in Section 4.

The term *error* describes a program action or state that violates the standard and that any given processor may fail to detect.

Implementation-defined means that a particular Pascal construct may differ between various implementations and that each implementation must specify how it implements that construct.

Implementation-dependent means that a particular construct varies between implementations and that an implementation does *not* have to specify how it implements that construct.

An *extension* is an additional construct usually not available in all implementations that does not in itself affect or invalidate the constructs of Standard Pascal. Implementations often support extensions in the form of additional predefined and predeclared constants, types, variables, procedures and functions.

A program that conforms to the standard must not depend on any implementation-dependent constructs or on any extensions. A portable program must, in addition, be very careful in its use of implementation-defined constructs (e.g., character set, or range of integer values).

4.   Symbols and Symbol Separators

A program is represented as a sequence of symbols arranged according to the rules of Pascal syntax. Adjacent symbols often are separated by symbol separators for purposes of readability. Symbols are categorized as the special symbols, identifiers, directives, numbers, labels, and character strings. Symbol separators are spaces, comments, and the ends of lines of the textual program representation.

$$SpecialSymbol = \text{"+"} \mid \text{"-"} \mid \text{"*"} \mid \text{"/"} \mid$$
$$\text{"="} \mid \text{"<>"} \mid \text{"<"} \mid \text{"<="} \mid \text{">"} \mid \text{">="} \mid$$
$$\text{"("} \mid \text{")"} \mid \text{"["} \mid \text{"]"} \mid \text{":="} \mid \text{"."} \mid \text{".."} \mid$$
$$\text{":"} \mid \text{" ; "} \mid \text{"↑"} \mid WordSymbol .$$

$$WordSymbol = \text{"div"} \mid \text{"mod"} \mid \text{"nil"} \mid \text{"in"} \mid \text{"or"} \mid \text{"and"} \mid$$
$$\text{"not"} \mid \text{"if"} \mid \text{"then"} \mid \text{"else"} \mid \text{"case"} \mid \text{"of"} \mid$$
$$\text{"repeat"} \mid \text{"until"} \mid \text{"while"} \mid \text{"do"} \mid \text{"for"} \mid$$
$$\text{"to"} \mid \text{"goto"} \mid \text{"downto"} \mid \text{"begin"} \mid \text{"end"} \mid$$
$$\text{"with"} \mid \text{"const"} \mid \text{"var"} \mid \text{"type"} \mid \text{"array"} \mid$$
$$\text{"record"} \mid \text{"set"} \mid \text{"file"} \mid \text{"function"} \mid$$
$$\text{"procedure"} \mid \text{"label"} \mid \text{"packed"} \mid \text{"program"} .$$

The following alternative representations are standard:

Reference	Alternative
↑	^ or @
[	(.
]	.)

Many of the symbols are constructed from letters and digits. Except within a character string, a lower-case letter is equivalent to the corresponding upper-case letter.

$$Letter = \text{"a"} \mid \text{"b"} \mid \text{"c"} \mid \text{"d"} \mid \text{"e"} \mid \text{"f"} \mid \text{"g"} \mid \text{"h"} \mid$$
$$\text{"i"} \mid \text{"j"} \mid \text{"k"} \mid \text{"l"} \mid \text{"m"} \mid \text{"n"} \mid \text{"o"} \mid \text{"p"} \mid$$
$$\text{"q"} \mid \text{"r"} \mid \text{"s"} \mid \text{"t"} \mid \text{"u"} \mid \text{"v"} \mid \text{"w"} \mid \text{"x"} \mid$$
$$\text{"y"} \mid \text{"z"} .$$

$$Digit = \text{"0"} \mid \text{"1"} \mid \text{"2"} \mid \text{"3"} \mid \text{"4"} \mid \text{"5"} \mid \text{"6"} \mid \text{"7"} \mid \text{"8"} \mid \text{"9"} .$$

Identifiers serve to denote constants, types, variables, procedures, functions, fields, and bounds. Directives are used in procedure and function declarations.

$$Identifier = Letter \{ Letter \mid Digit \} .$$
$$Directive = Letter \{ Letter \mid Digit \} .$$

The *spelling* of a word symbol, identifier, or directive is the entire sequence of specific letters and digits that it contains. No identifier or directive may have the same spelling as a word symbol.

Examples of identifiers (six distinct spellings):

```
FirstPlace    ord     ProcedureOrFunctionDeclaration
Elizabeth     John    ProcedureOrFunctionHeading
```

A specific identifier spelling is introduced by a declaration or definition to have a specific meaning, and that identifier spelling cannot have any other meaning within a region of the program text that is called the *scope* of that declaration or definition (see Section 10).

Numbers are expressed using the usual decimal notation. Unsigned integers and unsigned reals are, respectively, constants of the predefined types Integer and Real (see Section 6.1.2). The letter "e" preceding the scale factor in an unsigned real means "times 10 to the power." The maximum value that an unsigned integer may represent is the implementation-defined value of the predefined constant Maxint.

> *UnsignedNumber*   =   *UnsignedInteger* | *UnsignedReal* .
>
> *UnsignedInteger*   =   *DigitSequence* .
>
> *UnsignedReal*   =   *UnsignedInteger* "." *DigitSequence*
>   ["e" *ScaleFactor*] |
>   *UnsignedInteger* "e" *ScaleFactor* .
>
> *ScaleFactor*   =   [*Sign*] *UnsignedInteger* .
>
> *Sign*   =   "+" | "−" .
>
> *DigitSequence*   =   *Digit* { *Digit* } .

Examples of unsigned integers:

```
1     100     00100
```

Examples of unsigned reals:

```
0.1    0.1e0     87.35e+8    1E2
```

The signed numbers are the form that is acceptable for numeric input from textfiles (see Section 12).

> *SignedNumber*   =   *SignedInteger* | *SignedReal* .
>
> *SignedInteger*   =   [*Sign*] *UnsignedInteger* .
>
> *SignedReal*   =   [*Sign*] *UnsignedReal* .

Character strings are sequences of string elements enclosed in apostrophes. A string element represents an implementation-defined value of the predefined type Char, and consists either of two adjacent apostrophes or of any other implementation-defined character. Two distinct characters occurring as string elements must denote distinct values of type Char. The string element consisting of two apostrophes denotes the apostrophe character.

> *CharacterString*   =   "'" *StringElement* { *StringElement* } "'" .
>
> *StringElement*   =   "''" | *AnyCharacterExceptApostrophe* .

A character string is a constant of type Char if it has one string element; otherwise it is a constant of a string type (see Section 6.2.1) that has as many components as there are string elements.

   Note: A character string must be written on just one line of program text.

Examples of character strings:
```
'A'             ';'
'Pascal'        ''''
'This is a character string'
```

Symbol separators may be placed between any two adjacent symbols or before the first symbol of a program. At least one symbol separator must occur between two adjacent identifiers, directives, word symbols, labels, or numbers. A separator is a space, the end of a line of program text, or a comment. The meaning of a program is unaltered if a comment is replaced with a space.

> *Comment* = ("{" | "(*") { *CommentElement* } ("}" | "*)") .

A *CommentElement* is either an end of line or any sequence of characters not containing "}" or "*)".

   Notes: { ... *) and (* ... } are valid comments. The comment {(*) is equivalent to the comment {(}.

5.   Constants

A constant definition introduces a constant identifier to denote the value that is specified by the constant in the definition; the constant identifier being defined must not occur in the constant part of the definition. Constant definitions are collected into constant definition parts.

> *ConstantDefinitionPart*   =   ["const" *ConstantDefinition* ";"
>   { *ConstantDefinition* ";" }].
>
> *ConstantDefinition*   =   *Identifier* "=" *Constant* .

Constant   = [*Sign*] (*UnsignedNumber* |
                                ConstantIdentifier) | *CharacterString* .

ConstantIdentifier   = *Identifier* .

A constant identifier that is prefixed with a sign ("+" or "-") must denote a value of type Integer or Real.

There are three standard predefined constant identifiers: Maxint denotes an implementation-defined value of type Integer; false and true denote the values of type Boolean (see Section 6.1.2).

Example of a constant definition part:
```
const
   N = 20;
   SpeedOfLight = 2.998e8 { meters / second };
   PoleStar = 'Polaris';
   eps = 1E-6;
```

6. Types

A *type* determines the set of values that variables, expressions, functions, etc., possessing that type may assume. Rules of type *compatibility* determine how types may be used together in expressions, assignments, etc.

A type definition introduces a type identifier to denote a type; the type identifier being defined must not occur in the type part of the definition except as the domain type of a pointer type (see Section 6.3). Type definitions are collected into type definition parts. Section 6.4 gives an example of a type definition part.

TypeDefinitionPart   = ["type" *TypeDefinition* ";"
                          { *TypeDefinition* ";" }] .

TypeDefinition   = *Identifier* "=" *Type* .

TypeIdentifier   = *Identifier* .

Types are represented by the EBNF meta-identifier *Type*. If a type representation consists only of a type identifier, then it represents the same (existing) type that the type identifier denotes. If a type representation does not consist only of a type identifier, then it represents an entirely new type. Types are classified according to some of their properties:

Type = *SimpleType* | *StructuredType* | *PointerType* .

6.1. Simple Types

A simple type determines an ordered set of values, and is either the predefined *real* type or an *ordinal* type. A real type identifier is a type identifier that denotes the real type.

> *SimpleType* = *OrdinalType* | *RealTypeIdentifier* .
>
> *RealTypeIdentifier* = *TypeIdentifier* .

An ordinal type is distinguished (from the *real* type) by the one-to-one correspondence between its values and a set of *ordinal numbers*. The ordinal numbers for any ordinal type constitute an interval of the integers.

The following three predeclared functions apply to any ordinal value X:

ord(X)   yields the ordinal number corresponding to X; the result is of type Integer.

succ(X)   yields the successor of X. That is,

> succ(X) > X, and ord(succ(X)) = ord(X)+1

unless X is the largest value of its type, in which case succ(X) is an error.

pred(X)   yields the predecessor of X. That is,

> pred(X) < X, and ord(pred(X)) = ord(X)-1

unless X is the smallest value of its type, in which case pred(X) is an error.

Clearly, the ordering of the values of an ordinal type is the same as the ordering of their ordinal numbers.

An ordinal type either is an *enumerated* type or one of the predefined types Integer, Char, or Boolean, or else is a *subrange* of one of these.

> *OrdinalType* = *EnumeratedType* | *SubrangeType* | *OrdinalTypeIdentifier*.
>
> *OrdinalTypeIdentifier* = *TypeIdentifier* .

An ordinal type identifier is a type identifier that denotes an ordinal type.

6.1.1. Enumerated types. An enumerated type defines a set of entirely new values and introduces a constant identifier to denote each value.

> *EnumeratedType* = "(" *IdentifierList* ")" .
>
> *IdentifierList* = *Identifier* { "," *Identifier* } .

The first identifier denotes the smallest value, which has the ordinal number zero. Every other identifier in the list denotes the successor of the value denoted by the preceding identifier. That is, the constant identifiers are listed in order of increasing value.

Examples of enumerated types:
```
(Red, Orange, Yellow, Green, Blue)
(Club, Diamond, Heart, Spade)
(Monday, Tuesday, Wednesday, Thursday, Friday, Saturday, Sunday)
```

6.1.2. Predefined simple types. The following predefined type identifiers are standard in Pascal.

Real   determines an implementation-defined subset of the real numbers.

Integer   includes the set of integers having an absolute value less than or equal to the implementation-defined value of the predefined constant identifier Maxint. For any integer I, ord(I) = I.

Boolean   determines the set of truth values denoted by the predefined constant identifiers false and true. Note that
false < true and ord(false) = 0.

Char   determines an implementation-defined set of characters having implementation-defined ordinal numbers, such that:

(a) the digits '0','1',...,'9' are numerically ordered and consecutive (e.g., succ('0') = '1');

(b) if the lower-case letters ('a','b',...,'z') are present, they are alphabetically ordered (but not necessarily consecutive!); and

(c) if the upper-case letters (A','B',...,'Z') are present, they are alphabetically ordered (but not necessarily consecutive!).

6.1.3. Subrange types. The set of values determined by a subrange type is a subset of the values of another ordinal type that is called the *host* type of the subrange type. The subrange type specifies the smallest and largest value, and includes every value between them.

> *SubrangeType* = *Constant* ".." *Constant* .

Both constants must possess the host type. The first constant specifies the smallest value, and must be less than or equal to the second constant which specifies the largest value.

Examples of subrange types:
```
1..N
-10 .. +10
Monday..Friday
```

6.2 Structured Types

A structured type is characterized by the type(s) of its components and by its structuring method. Moreover, a structured type may contain an indication of the preferred data representation. If a structured type is prefixed with the symbol packed, this has no effect on the meaning of a program (with two exceptions); rather it is a hint to the compiler that storage of values of that type should be economized even at the price of some loss in efficiency of access, and even if this may expand the code necessary for expressing access to components of the structure. The two exceptions are that string types (see Section 6.2.1) are always packed, and that an actual variable parameter (see Section 11.3) must not be a component of a packed structured variable. If a component of a packed structured type also possesses a structured type, the component's type is packed only if the symbol packed is explicitly given in the component's type representation.

> *StructuredType*   = ["packed"] *UnpackedStructuredType* |
>   *StructuredTypeIdentifier* .
> *UnpackedStructuredType* = *ArrayType* | *RecordType* | *SetType* |
>   *FileType* .
> *StructuredTypeIdentifier* = *TypeIdentifier* .

A structured type identifier is a type identifier that denotes a structured type.

6.2.1 Array types. An array type is a structure consisting of a fixed number of components which are all of the same type, called the *component type*. The components are in a one-to-one correspondence with the values of the *index type*.

ArrayType   = "array" "[" IndexType { "," IndexType } "]"
                   "of" ComponentType .

IndexType   = OrdinalType .

ComponentType   = Type .

More than one index type may be specified, as in

```
packed array [T1, T2, ..., Tn] of C,
```

and this is simply an abbreviation for the notation

```
packed array [T1] of array [T2, ..., Tn] of C.
```

These two notations would also be equivalent if neither were prefixed with packed.

Examples of array types:
```
array [1..100] of Real
array [1..10, 1..20] of 0.99
array [Boolean] of Color
array [Size] of packed array ['a'..'z'] of Boolean
```

Each value of an array type is a functional (many-to-one) mapping from the entire set of index values to the set of values of the component type.

An array type is called a *string type* if it is packed, if it has as its component type the predefined type Char and if it has as its index type a subrange of Integer from 1 to n, for n greater than 1. The character strings (see Section 4) are constants of string types.

Examples:
```
packed array [1..StringLength] of Char
packed array [1..2] of Char
```

6.2.2. Record types. A record type has a fixed number of components, possibly of different types. The specific components and their types, and the values of the record type, are determined by the *field list* of the record type.

RecordType   = "record" *FieldList* "end" .

FieldList   = [(*FixedPart* [";" *VariantPart*] |
                       VariantPart) [";"]] .

FixedPart   = *RecordSection* [";" *RecordSection* } .

RecordSection   = *IdentifierList* ":" *Type* .

FieldIdentifier = *Identifier* .

A field list may contain a *fixed part,* which specifies a fixed number of components called *fields.* A record section introduces each of the identifiers in its list to be a field identifier possessing the type given in the record section. The scope of a field identifier extends over its record type, as well as field designators and with statements where it may be used (see Sections 7.2.2, 9.2.4, and 10.2). Thus each field identifier spelling must be unique within a record type.

Examples of record types with only fixed parts:
```
packed record
    Year: 1900..2100;
    Month: 1..12;
    Day: 1..31
end

record
    Firstname, Lastname:
        packed array [1..32] of Char;
    Age: 0..99;
    Married: Boolean
end
```

A field list may also contain a *variant part,* which specifies one or more *variants.* The structure and values of a variant are specified by its field list.

VariantPart = "case" *VariantSelector* "of" *Variant* { ";" *Variant* } .

Variant = *Constant* { "," *Constant* } ":" "(" *FieldList* ")" .

VariantSelector = [*TagField* ":"] *TagType* .

TagType = *OrdinalTypeIdentifier* .

TagField = *Identifier* .

A constant that prefixes a variant must denote a value of the tag type. Each such value must appear once and only once for a given variant part. If a tag field occurs in a variant selector, then it introduces its identifier as a field identifier to denote a field possessing the tag type.

Only one variant of a given variant part can be *active* at a given time. If there is a tag field, the variant that is prefixed by the value of the tag field is the active variant. If there is no tag field, then the active variant is the one possessing the most recently accessed component.

A value of a field list determines a value of each field specified in the fixed part and a value of the variant part. A value of a variant part consists of an indication of which variant is active, a value of the tag field (if any), and a value of the active variant.

Examples of record types with variant parts:
```
record
case NameKnown: Boolean of
   false: ( );
   true:  (Name: packed array [1..NameMax] of Char)
end

record
   X, Y: Real;
   Area: Real;
case S: Shape of
   Triangle:  ( Side: Real;
                Inclination, Angle1, Angle2: Angle
              );
   Rectangle: ( Side1, Side2: Real;
                Skew, Angle3: Angle
              );
   Circle:    ( Diameter: Real )
end
```

6.2.3. Set types. A set type determines as its set of values the powerset of the set of values of the *base type*. That is, each value of a set type is a set that contains zero or more elements (components), and each element is a value of the base type.

SetType = "set" "of" *BaseType* .

BaseType = *OrdinalType* .

Examples of set types:
```
set of Char
packed set of 0..11
```

6.2.4. File types. A file type is structured as a sequence of components having a single type (the component type), together with a position in the sequence and a mode that indicates whether the file is being generated or inspected. The number of components in the sequence, called the *length* of the file, is not fixed by the file type. A file is called *empty* if its length is zero.

FileType = "file" "of" *ComponentType* .

The component type of a file type must be an assignable type (see Section 6.5). A file that is in *inspection* mode may be positioned at any component of the sequence or at the *end-of-file* position. A file that is in *generation* mode is always positioned at end-of-file. File values are manipulated by the predeclared file-handling procedures and functions (see Section 11).

The predefined structured type identifier Text represents a special file type in which the sequence is structured as zero or more *lines*. A line consists of zero or more characters (values of type Char) followed by a special *end-of-line* marker. A variable of type Text is called a *textfile*. If a nonempty textfile is in inspection mode then there is always an end-of-line immediately preceding the end-of-file position. There are several additional predeclared procedures and functions for manipulating textfiles (see Sections 11.5 and 12).

6.3. Pointer Types

A pointer type is distinguished from the structured and simple types in that its set of values is *dynamic;* i.e., values of a pointer type are created and destroyed during program execution. The set of values of a pointer type always contains a special value, represented by nil. Every other value in the set must be created by a program using the predeclared procedure New (see Section 11.4.2); such values are called *identifying values* because each one identifies a variable, the so-called *identified variable* (see Section 7.3). An identified variable possesses the *domain type* of the pointer type. An identifying value and its identified variable can be destroyed using the predeclared procedure Dispose (see Section 11.4.2). All identifying values created by a program cease to exist when the program terminates.

PointerType = "↑" *DomainType* | *PointerTypeIdentifier* .

DomainType = *TypeIdentifier* .

PointerTypeIdentifier = *TypeIdentifier* .

6.4.   Example of a Type Definition Part

```
type
    Natural = 0..Maxint;
    Color = (Red, Yellow, Green, Blue);
    Hue = set of Color;
    Shape = (Triangle, Rectangle, Circle);
    Year = 1900..2100;
    Card = array [1..80] of Char;
    String18 = packed array [1..18] of Char;
    Complex = record Re, Im: Real end;
    PersonPointer = ↑ Person;
    Relationship = (Married, Coupled, Single);
    Person =
        record
            Name, Firstname: String18;
            BirthYear: Year;
            Sex: (Male, Female);
            Father, Mother: PersonPointer;
            Friends, Children: file of PersonPointer;
            ExRelationshipCount: Natural;
        case Status: Relationship of
            Married, Coupled: (SignificantOther: PersonPointer);
            Single: ( )
        end;
    MatrixIndex = 1..N;
    SquareMatrix = array [MatrixIndex, MatrixIndex] of Real;
```

6.5.   Type Compatibility

Two types are said to be *compatible* if any of the following four
conditions is true.

(a)   They are the same type.

(b)   One is a subrange of the other, or both are subranges of the
same host type.

(c)   Both are set types, their base types are compatible, and
either both are packed or neither is packed.

(d)   Both are string types with the same number of components.

A type is called *assignable* if it is neither a file type nor a
structured type with a component type that is not assignable.

A value possessing type T2 is called *assignment-compatible* with a type T1 if any of the following four conditions is true.

(a)   T1 and T2 are the same assignable type.

(b)   T1 is Real and T2 is Integer.

(c)   T1 and T2 are compatible ordinal types or compatible set types, and the value is a member of the set of values determined by T1.

(d)   T1 and T2 are compatible string types.

Wherever assignment-compatibility is required, and T1 and T2 are either compatible ordinal types or compatible set types, it is an error if the value is not a member of the set of values determined by T1.

7.   Variables

A variable possesses a type that is determined by its declaration, and may take on values only of that type.

A variable is *undefined* if it does not have a value of its type. A variable is *totally undefined* if it is undefined and further if every component of the (structured) variable is totally undefined. When a variable is created it is totally undefined. A variable declared in a block is created when the block is activated and destroyed when the activation is terminated (see Section 10). An identified variable is created or destroyed, respectively, by the predeclared procedure New or Dispose (see Sections 6.3 and 11.4).

A variable declaration introduces one or more variable identifiers and the type that each one possesses. Variable declarations are collected into variable declaration parts.

VariableDeclarationPart   =   ["var" *VariableDeclaration* ";"
                                 { *VariableDeclaration* ";" }] .

VariableDeclaration   =   *IdentifierList* ":" *Type* .

VariableIdentifier   =   *Identifier* .

Example of a variable declaration part:
```
var
    W, X, Y: Real;
    Z: Complex;
    I, J: Integer;
    K: 0..9;
```

```
P, Q: Boolean;
Operator: (Plus, Minus, Times);
GrayScale: array [0..63] of Real;
VideoPotential: array [Color, Boolean] of Complex;
Light: Color;
F: file of Char;
Hue1, Hue2: set of Hue;
P1, P2: PersonPointer;
A, B, C: SquareMatrix;
Minneapolis, Zuerich: packed record
                          Area: Real;
                          Population: Natural;
                          Capital: Boolean
                      end;
```

An access to a variable is represented by the EBNF meta-identifier *Variable*.

Variable = EntireVariable | ComponentVariable |
            IdentifiedVariable | BufferVariable .

7.1. Entire Variables

An entire variable represents the variable that is denoted by the variable identifier.

EntireVariable = VariableIdentifier .

Examples of entire variables:
```
Input
P1
VideoPotential
```

7.2. Component Variables

A component of a structured variable is also a variable; a component variable represents an access to a component of a structured variable. The syntax of the component variable depends on the type of the structured variable.

ComponentVariable = IndexedVariable | FieldDesignator .

An access or reference to a component of a structured variable implies an access or reference to the structured variable.

7.2.1. Indexed variables. An indexed variable represents a component of an array variable. An array variable is a variable that possesses an array type.

> *IndexedVariable = ArrayVariable "[" Index { "," Index } "]" .*
>
> *Index = OrdinalExpression .*
>
> *ArrayVariable = Variable .*

The component accessed is the one that corresponds to the value of the index expression, which must be assignment-compatible (see Section 6.5) with the index type when the access occurs. When there are multiple index expressions, the order of their evaluation is implementation-dependent.

Examples:
```
GrayScale[12]
GrayScale[I+J]
VideoPotential[Red, True]
```

When more than one index appears, as in

```
VideoPotential[Red, True],
```

it is simply an abbreviation for the notation

```
VideoPotential[Red][True].
```

7.2.2. Field designators. A field designator denotes a field of a record variable. A record variable is a variable that possesses a record type.

> *FieldDesignator = [RecordVariable "."] FieldIdentifier .*
>
> *RecordVariable = Variable .*

The field that is denoted is the one corresponding to the field identifier; only the field identifiers belonging to the record type of the record variable may appear. The record variable and the "." may be omitted inside of a with statement (see Section 9.2.4) that lists the record variable.

Examples of field designators:
```
Z.Re
VideoPotential[Red,True].Im
P2↑.Mother
```

When a variant of a record variable becomes inactive, all of the components of the variant become totally undefined. If there is no tag field in a variant part, then an access to a component of a variant makes that variant active and the other variants inactive. It is an error if a variant is or becomes inactive while there is an access or reference to any of its components. When a tag field is undefined, no variants of that variant part are active. A tag field must not be an actual variable parameter.

7.3. Identified Variables

An identified variable denotes the variable that is identified by the value of a pointer variable. A pointer variable is a variable that possesses a pointer type.

> *IdentifiedVariable = PointerVariable "↑" .*
>
> *PointerVariable = Variable .*

An access to an identified variable implies an access to the pointer variable, at which time it is an error if the pointer variable is undefined or has the value nil. It is an error if an identifying pointer value is destroyed when a reference to the variable that the value identifies exists.

Examples of identified variables:
```
p1↑
p1↑.Father↑
p1↑.Friends↑↑
```

7.4. Buffer Variables

A file variable is a variable that possesses a file type. With every file variable there is associated a so-called buffer variable.

> *BufferVariable = FileVariable "↑" .*
>
> *FileVariable = Variable .*

If the file variable possesses the type Text, then the buffer variable possesses the type Char; otherwise the buffer variable possesses the component type of the file type possessed by the file variable. The buffer variable is used to access the current component of the file variable. It is an error to perform any operation that alters the sequence, position, or mode of a file variable when a reference to the buffer variable exists. An access or reference to a buffer variable implies an access or reference to the associated file variable.

Predeclared procedures and functions that manipulate file variables are described in Sections 11.4, 11.5, and 12.

For a textfile F when eoln(F) becomes true (see Section 11.5.2), the buffer variable F↑ takes on the char value space (' '). Thus eoln(F) is the only way to detect an end-of-line marker on F.

Examples of buffer variables:
```
Input↑
P1↑.Friends↑
P1↑.Friends↑↑.Children↑
```

8. Expressions

An *expression* denotes a rule of computation that yields a value when the expression is evaluated, except when the expression activates a function and that activation is terminated by a goto statement (see Sections 9.1.3 and 10). The value that is yielded depends upon the values of the constants, bounds, and variables in the expression and also upon the operators and functions that the expression invokes.

Expression = SimpleExpression [RelationalOperator SimpleExpression].

SimpleExpression = [Sign] Term { AddingOperator Term } .

Term = Factor { MultiplyingOperator Factor } .

Factor = UnsignedConstant | BoundIdentifier | Variable |
   SetConstructor | FunctionDesignator |
   "not" Factor | "(" Expression ")" .

UnsignedConstant = UnsignedNumber | CharacterString |
      ConstantIdentifier | "nil" .

SetConstructor = "[" [ElementDescription { ","
      ElementDescription }] "]" .

ElementDescription = OrdinalExpression [".." OrdinalExpression] .

FunctionDesignator = FunctionIdentifier [ActualParameterList] .

RelationalOperator = "=" | "<>" | "<" | "<=" | ">" | ">=" | "in" .

AddingOperator = "+" | "−" | "or" .

MultiplyingOperator = "" | "/" | "div" | "mod" | "and" .*

An ordinal expression is an expression that possesses an ordinal type. A Boolean expression or integer expression is an ordinal expression that possesses the type `Boolean` or `Integer`, respectively.

> *OrdinalExpression* = *Expression* .
>
> *BooleanExpression* = *OrdinalExpression* .
> *IntegerExpression* = *OrdinalExpression* .

8.1. Operands

A multiplying operator in a term has two operands: the part of the term that precedes the operator, and the factor that immediately follows the operator. An adding operator in a simple expression has two operands: the part of the simple expression that precedes the operator, and the term that immediately follows the operator. The two operands of a relational operator are the simple expressions that immediately precede and follow the operator. The operand of a sign in a simple expression is the term that immediately follows the sign. The operand of `not` in a factor is the factor following `not`.

The order of evaluation of the operands of an operator is implementation-dependent. A standard program must not make any assumption about this order. The left operand might be evaluated before or after the right operand, or they might be evaluated in parallel. In fact, sometimes one operand might not be evaluated at all for some values of the other operand. For example, evaluating the expression (j `*` (i div j)) when j is zero might yield zero on one implementation, where on another implementation it might be an error due to the division by zero.

The type of a factor is derived from the type of its constituent (e.g., variable or function). If the constituent's type is a subrange, then the type of the factor is the host type of the subrange; if the constituent's type is a set type with a subrange as its base type, then the type of the factor is a set type with the host type of that subrange type as its base type; otherwise, the type of the factor is the same as the type of the constituent.

The symbol `nil` possesses every pointer type and represents the nil value.

A set constructor denotes a set value. If there are no element descriptions in the set constructor, then it denotes the empty set that is a value of every set type. Otherwise, the elements of the set value are described by the element descriptions in the set constructor. All expressions in the element descriptions of a set constructor must have the same type, which is the base type of the type of the set constructor. The type of a set constructor is both packed and unpacked, and is compatible with any other set type that has a compatible base type.

An element description consisting of a single expression describes the element that has the value denoted by the expression. An element description of the form a..b describes an element for each value x that satisfies a <= x <= b. If a > b, then a..b denotes no elements. The order of evaluation of the expressions in an element description and the order of evaluation of the element descriptions in a set constructor are implementation-dependent.

The evaluation of a factor consisting of a variable specifies an access to the variable and denotes the value of the variable; it is an error if the variable is undefined.

The evaluation of a factor consisting of a function designator specifies an activation of the function that is denoted by the function identifier (see Section 10.3). Any actual parameters are substituted for their corresponding formal parameters (see Section 11.3). Upon completion of the activation's algorithm, the factor denotes the value of the result of the activation; it is an error if the result is undefined.

8.2 Operators

The rules of composition specify operator *precedences* according to four classes of operators. The operator not has the highest precedence, followed by the so-called multiplying operators, then the so-called adding operators, and finally, with the lowest precedence, the relational operators. Sequences of operators of the same precedence are executed from left to right. The rules of precedence are reflected in the EBNF rules for *Expression, Simple-Expression, Term,* and *Factor* (above).

Operators are also classified as arithmetic, Boolean, set, and relational operators according to their operand and result types.

8.2.1. Arithmetic operators. An arithmetic operator takes integer or real operands and yields an integer or real results.

The following table summarizes operators that take one operand, i.e., the signs.

Operator	Operation	Type of Operand	Type of Result
+	identity	Integer or Real	same as operand
−	sign inversion	Integer or Real	same as operand

The following table summarizes the operators that take two operands.

Operator	Operation	Type of Operands	Type of Result
+	addition	Integer or Real	Integer or Real
–	subtraction	Integer or Real	Integer or Real
*	multiplication	Integer or Real	Integer or Real
/	division	Integer or Real	Real
div	division	Integer	Integer
mod	modulo	Integer	Integer

The result type of addition, subtraction and multiplication is Integer if both operands are Integer, otherwise it is Real.

Evaluation of a term of the form x / y is an error if y is zero.

Evaluation of a term of the form x div y is an error if y is zero; otherwise the term yields the value satisfying the following two rules:

(a) abs(x) – abs(y) < abs((x div y) * y) <= abs(x), and

(b) x div y = 0 if abs(x) < abs(y), otherwise x div y is positive if x and y have the same sign and is negative if x and y have different signs.

Evaluation of a term of the form x mod y is an error if y is less than or equal to zero; otherwise there is an integer k such that x mod y satisfies the following relation:

0 <= x mod y = x – k * y < y.

For any integer operators, if both operands are in the range –Maxint..Maxint and if the correct result is in that range, then a standard implementation must yield the correct result. However, if the operands or result is not in the range –Maxint..Maxint, an implementation may choose either to perform the operation correctly or to treat the operation as an error.

Any operator or predeclared function (see Section 11.5) that yields a real result must always be considered to be approximate, not exact. The accurancy of real operations and predeclared functions is implementation-defined.

8.2.2. Boolean Operators. The Boolean operators are summarized by the following table.

Operator	Operation	Type of Operands	Type of Result
not	logical "not"	Boolean	Boolean
and	logical "and"	Boolean	Boolean
or	logical "or"	Boolean	Boolean

8.2.3. Set Operators. The set operators are summarized by the following table. The two operands must always possess compatible types (see Section 6.5). The result type is packed if both operand types are packed, and is unpacked if both operand types are unpacked.

Operator	Operation	Type of Operands	Type of Result
+	set union	set of T	set of T
−	set difference	set of T	set of T
*	set intersection	set of T	set of T

8.2.4. Relational Operators. The relational operators are summarized by the following table. With the exception of the operator in, the types possessed by the operands either must be compatible, or one must be Real and the other must be Integer. For in, the first (left) operand must possess an ordinal type that is compatible with the base type of the set type possessed by the second operand.

The expression x <= y where x and y are sets yields true if every member of x is a member of y, i.e., if x is a subset of y.

The ordering of compatible strings is according to the ordering of the values of type Char (see Section 6.1.2).

Operator	Operation	Type of Operands	Type of Result
=	equality	simple, pointer, set, or string	Boolean
<>	inequality	simple, pointer, set, or string	Boolean
<=	less than or equal	simple or string	Boolean
<=	set inclusion	set	Boolean
>=	greater than or equal	simple or string	Boolean
>=	set inclusion	set	Boolean
<	less than	simple or string	Boolean
>	greater than	simple or string	Boolean
in	set membership	ordinal and set	Boolean

Examples of factors:
```
X
15
(W + X + Y)
sin(X+Y)
[Red, Light, Green]
[1, 5, 10..19, 60]
not P
```

Examples of terms:
```
X * Y
I/(1-I)
Q and not P
(X <= Y) and (Y < W)
```

Examples of simple expressions:
```
X + GrayScale[2 * I]
-X
P or Q
Hue1 + Hue2
I*J + 1
```

Examples of expressions:
```
X = 1.5
P <= Q
(I < J) = (J < K)
Light in Hue1
```

9. Statements

Statements denote algorithmic actions, and are said to be *executable*. A statement may be prefixed by a label which can be referred to by goto statements. Statements are collected into statement parts.

> *Statement* = [*Label* ":"] (*SimpleStatement* | *StructuredStatement*) .
>
> *StatementPart* = *CompoundStatement* .

9.1. Simple Statements

A simple statement is a statement of which no part constitutes another statement. The empty statement consists of no symbols and denotes no action.

> *SimpleStatement* = *EmptyStatement* | *AssignmentStatement* |
>   *ProcedureStatement* | *GotoStatement* .
>
> *EmptyStatement* = .

9.1.1. Assignment statements.

The assignment statement serves to access the variable or function-activation result and to replace its current value by the value obtained by evaluating the expression.

> *AssignmentStatement* = (*Variable* | *FunctionIdentifier*) ":=" *Expression* .

The value of the expression must be assignment-compatible (see Section 6.5) with the type of the variable or function identifier. The order of accessing the variable or result and evaluating the expression is implementation-dependent. The access to the variable establishes a reference to the variable that exists until the value is assigned.

Examples of assignment statements:
```
X := Y + GrayScale[31]
P := (1 <= I) and (I < 100)
I := sqr(K) - (I*J)
Hue2 := [Blue, succ(C)]
```

9.1.2. Procedure statements.

A procedure statement serves to activate the procedure denoted by the procedure identifier. The procedure statement may contain a list of *actual parameters* which are substituted in place of their corresponding *formal parameters* defined in the procedure declaration (see 11.1).

> *ProcedureStatement* = *ProcedureIdentifier* [*ActualParameterList* |
> *WriteParameterList*] .

If the procedure identifier denotes the standard procedure Write or Writeln, then the actual parameters must follow the syntax specified for a *WriteParameterList*. If the procedure identifier denotes any other predeclared procedure, then the actual parameters must satisfy the rules stated in Sections 11.4 and 12.

Examples of procedure statements:
```
Next
Transpose(A,N,N)
Bisect(Fct, -1.0, +1.0, X)
Writeln(Output, ' Title' )
```

9.1.3. Goto statements.

A goto statement serves to indicate that further processing should continue at another part of the program, namely at the program-point denoted by the label (see Sections 10.1 and 10.3).

> *GotoStatement* = "goto" *Label* .

The statement that is prefixed by a label and each goto statement that refers to that label must satisfy one of the following two rules.

(a)   The statement either must contain the goto statement or else must be one of the statements in a statement sequence (see Section 9.2) that contains the goto statement.

(b)   The statement must be one of the statements in the statement sequence of the compound statement of the statement part of the block where the label is declared, and the goto statement must be contained in the procedure and function declaration part of that block (see Section 10.1).

The effect of these rules is to prevent goto statements transferring control into a structured statement or a procedure or function from outside. The first rule also disallows a goto transferring control between "branches" of a conditional statement.

If the program-point and the goto statement are not in the same statement part, then every activation that does not satisfy one of the following two conditions is terminated (see Section 10.3).

(a)   The activation contains the program-point.

(b)   The activation contains the activation-point of another activation that is not terminated (i.e., that satisfies one of these two conditions).

9.2. Structured Statements

Structured statements are constructs composed of other statements which have to be executed either in sequence (compound statement), conditionally (conditional statements), repeatedly (repetitive statements), or within an expanded scope (with statement).

> *StructuredStatement = CompoundStatement | ConditionalStatement |*
> *RepetitiveStatement | WithStatement .*

A statement sequence is a sequence of statements that are to be executed in the sequence that they are written, except where a goto statement indicates otherwise.

> *StatementSequence = Statement { ";" Statement } .*

Statement sequences are used in compound statements (Section 9.2.1), and repeat statements (Section 9.2.3.2).

9.2.1. Compound statements. A compound statement specifies the execution of the statement sequence. The symbols `begin` and `end` act as statement brackets.

> *CompoundStatement = "begin" StatementSequence "end" .*

Examples of compound statements:
```
begin   end
begin   W := X; X := Y; Y := W   end
```

9.2.2. Conditional statements. A conditional statement selects for execution one of its component statements.

> *ConditionalStatement = IfStatement | CaseStatement .*

9.2.2.1. If statements. The if statement specifies that the statement following the symbol `then` be executed only if the Boolean expression yields true. If it is false, then the statement following the symbol `else`, if any, is to be executed.

> *IfStatement = "if" BooleanExpression "then" Statement*
> *["else" Statement] .*

Note: The syntactic ambiguity arising from the construct

```
if e1 then if e2 then s1 else s2
```

is resolved by interpreting the construct as equivalent to

```
if e1 then
    begin if e2 then s1 else s2 end
```

Examples of if statements:
```
if X < 1.5 then W := X + Y else W := 1.5
if P1 <> nil then P1 := P1↑.Father
```

9.2.2.2. Case statements. The case statement consists of an ordinal expression (the case index) and a list of statements, each being prefixed by one or more constants of the type of the case index. It specifies that the one statement be executed that is prefixed by the value of the case index; it is an error if no constant denoting that value prefixes any statement. Each value must be specified by at most one case constant.

> *CaseStatement = "case" CaseIndex "of" Case { ";" Case } [";"] "end" .*

CaseIndex = OrdinalExpression .

Case = Constant { "," Constant } ":" Statement .

Examples of case statements:

```
case Operator of
    Plus:   W := X + Y;
    Minus:  W := X - Y;
    Times:  W := X * Y
end

case I of
    1:  Y := sin(X);
    2:  Y := cos(X);
    3:  Y := exp(X);
    4:  Y := ln(X)
end

case P1↑.Status of
    Married:  P1 := P1↑.SignificantOther;
    Coupled:  P2 := P1↑.SignificantOther;
    Single:
end
```

9.2.3. Repetitive statements. Repetitive statements specify that certain statements are to be executed repeatedly. If the number of repetitions is known beforehand, i.e., before the repetitions are started, the for statement is often the appropriate construct; otherwise the while or repeat statement should be used.

RepetitiveStatement = WhileStatement | RepeatStatement | ForStatement

9.2.3.1. While statement.

WhileStatement = "while" BooleanExpression "do" Statement .

The statement is repeatedly executed until the expression becomes false. If its value is false at the beginning, the statement is not executed at all. The while statement

```
while B do S
```

is equivalent to

```
if B then begin S;  while B do S  end
```

unless S contains a labelled statement.

Examples of while statements:
```
while GrayScale[I] < X do I := succ(I)

while I > 0 do
   begin
      if odd(I) then Y:= Y * X;
      I := I div 2;
      X := sqr(X)
   end

while not eof(F) do
   begin  P(F↑); Get(F)  end
```

9.2.3.2. Repeat statements.

> *RepeatStatement* = "repeat" *StatementSequence* "until"
>   *BooleanExpression* .

The statement sequence is repeatedly executed (and at least once) until the expression becomes true. The repeat statement

```
repeat S until B
```

is equivalent to

```
begin  S;  if not B then repeat S until B  end
```

unless S contains a labelled statement.

Examples of repeat statements:
```
repeat  K := I mod J;  I := J;  J := K  until J = 0

repeat
   P(F↑);
   Get(F)
until eof(F)
```

9.2.3.3. For statements. The for statement indicates that a statement is to be repeatedly executed while a progression of values is assigned to a variable that is called the *control variable* of the for statement.

> *ForStatement* = "for" *ControlVariable* ":=" *InitialValue*
>   ("to" | "downto") *FinalValue* "do" *Statement* .
>
> *ControlVariable* = *VariableIdentifier* .
>
> *InitialValue* = *OrdinalExpression* .
>
> *FinalValue* = *OrdinalExpression* .

The control variable must be local to the block (see Section 10.2) whose statement part contains the for statement, and must possess an ordinal type that is compatible with the types of the initial value and final value.

A statement S is said to *threaten* a variable V if any of the following conditions are true.

(a) S is an assignment statement that assigns to V.

(b) S contains V occurring as an actual variable parameter (see Section 11.3.2.2).

(c) S is a procedure statement that activates the predeclared procedure Read or Readln and V is one of its actual parameters.

(d) S is a for statement and V is its control variable.

No statement inside the for statement must threaten the control variable. Also, no procedure or function declared local to the block in which the control variable is declared may contain a statement that threatens the control variable. These rules ensure that the repeated statement cannot alter the value of the control variable.

Let T1 and T2 be new variables (not otherwise accessible) possessing the same type as V, and let P be a new variable possessing type Boolean. Then with the exceptions noted in comments, the following equivalences hold.

```
for V := el to e2 do S
```

is equivalent to

```
begin
    T1 := el; T2 := e2;
    if T1 <= T2 then
        begin
            { T2 must be assignment-compatible with the type of V }
            V := T1; P:= false;
            repeat
                S;
                if V = T2 then P := true else V := succ(V)
            until P
        end
    { V is undefined }
end
```

and

```
        for V := e1 downto e2 do S
```

is equivalent to

```
    begin
        T1 := e1; T2 := e2;
        if T1 >= T2 then
            begin
                { T2 must be assignment-compatible with the type of V }
                V := T1; P := false;
                repeat
                    S;
                    if V = T2 then P := true else V := pred(V)
                until P
            end
        { V is undefined }
    end
```

Examples of for statements:

```
    for I := 1 to 63 do
        if GrayScale[I] > 0.5 then write ('*') else write (' ')

    for I := 1 to n do
        for J := 1 to n do
            begin
                X := 0;
                for K := 1 to n do X := X + A[I,K] * B[K,J];
                C[I,J] := X
            end

    for Light := Red to pred(Light) do
        if Light in Hue2 then Q(Light)
```

9.2.4. With statements. A with statement accesses and establishes a reference to each record variable in its list, and then executes the component statement. The reference exists during the execution of the component statement.

WithStatement = "with" *RecordVariableList* "do" *Statement* .

RecordVariableList = *RecordVariable* { "," *RecordVariable* } .

The scope (see Section 10.2) of each of the field identifiers of the type of a (single) record variable listed in a with statement is extended to include the component statement. Within this extended scope, the field identifier can occur in a field designator without respecifying the record variable, and will denote the appropriate field of the referenced variable.

The notation

```
with r1, r2, ..., rn do S
```

is an abbreviation for the notation

```
with r1 do
   with r1 do
      ...
         with rn do S
```

Example of with statement:
```
with Date do
   if Month = 12 then
      begin  Month := 1;  Year := succ(Year)  end
   else Month := succ(Month)
```

This is equivalent to

```
if Date.Month = 12 then
   begin  Date.Month := 1;  Date.Year := succ(Date.Year)  end
else Date.Month := succ(Date.Month)
```

10.   Blocks, Scope, and Activations

Blocks are the basis for constructing programs (see Section 13) and procedures and functions (see Section 11). The *scope* rules determine where an identifier spelling that is introduced in a particular place can be used, based on the static (textual) program structure. The *activation* rules determine what entity (e.g., variable) is denoted by a particular identifier or label, based on the dynamic (execution) program structure.

10.1.   Blocks

A block consists of several definition and declaration parts, any of which may be empty, and a statement part.

Block =   *LabelDeclarationPart*
            ConstantDefinitionPart
            TypeDefinitionPart
            VariableDeclarationPart
            ProcedureAndFunctionDeclarationPart
            StatementPart .

The label declaration part introduces one or more labels, each of which must prefix one statement in the statement part.

> *LabelDeclarationPart* = ["label" *DigitSequence* { ","
> *DigitSequence* } ";"] .
>
> *Label*   = *DigitSequence* .

The *spelling* of a label is the apparent integral value that its digit sequence describes in the usual decimal notation; the value must not exceed 9999.

10.2. Scope

A definition or declaration introduces a spelling of an identifier or a label and associates the spelling with a specific meaning (e.g., a variable identifier). The parts of a program in which every occurrence of that spelling must take on that meaning are collectively called the *scope* of the introduction (definition or declaration). The occurrence of a spelling in its introduction must precede every other occurrence of that spelling within the scope of the introduction, with one exception. The exception is that a type-identifier spelling may occur as the domain type of a pointer type (see Section 6.3) anywhere in the type definition part that contains the spelling's introduction.

Each introduction is effective for some region of the program, as described below. The scope of the introduction is that region less any enclosed region for which another introduction of the same spelling is effective.

The following introductions are effective for the block in which the introduction occurs: a label in a label declaration part; a constant identifier in a constant definition part or in an enumerated type; a type identifier in a type definition part; a variable identifier in a variable declaration part; a procedure identifier in a procedure declaration (see Section 11.1); and a function identifier in a function declaration (see Section 11.2). These labels and identifiers are said to be *local* to the block.

The implicit introduction of standard predefined and predeclared identifiers is effective for a region that surrounds every program.

The introduction of a field identifier in a record type is effective for each of the following regions:

(a)   the record type itself;

(b)   the component statement of a with statement where the record variable of the with statement possesses that record type; and

(c)   the field-identifier part of a field designator where the record-variable part of the field designator possesses that record type.

In the case of (c), the field-identifier part is excluded from all other enclosing scopes.

The introduction of a parameter identifier in a parameter list (see Section 11.3.1) is effective for the parameter list. Furthermore, if the parameter list is in the procedure heading of a procedure declaration or in the function heading of a function declaration, then a variable identifier, bound identifier, procedure identifier, or function identifier that corresponds to the parameter identifier is introduced effective for the block of that procedure declaration or function declaration.

10.3. Activations

An activation of a program (see Section 13), or a procedure or function (see Section 11) is an activation of the block of the program, procedure, or function.

An activation of a block is said to *contain* the following entities, which exist until the activation terminates.

(a)   An *algorithm* that is specified by the statement part of the block; the algorithm commences when the block is activated, and completion of the algorithm terminates the activation. (The activation might instead terminate due to a goto statement — see Section 9.1.3.)

(b)   A *program-point* in the algorithm corresponding to each label that prefixes a statement in the statement part of the block. Each appearance of that label in a goto statement within the activation denotes that program-point.

(c)   A *variable* for each variable identifier that is local to the block; when the algorithm commences, the variable is totally undefined unless the variable identifier is a program parameter. Each appearance of that variable identifier within the activation denotes that variable.

(d) A *procedure* for each procedure identifier that is local to the block; the procedure has the block and formal parameters of the procedure declaration that introduced the procedure identifier. Each occurrence of that procedure identifier within the activation denotes that procedure.

(e) A *function* for each function identifier that is local to the block; the function has the block, formal parameters, and result type of the function declaration that introduced the function identifier. Each occurrence of that function identifier within the activation denotes that function.

(f) A *variable* for each variable identifier that is a formal value parameter identifier for the block; when the algorithm commences, the variable has the value of the corresponding actual parameter in the procedure statement or function designator that activated the procedure or function. Each occurrence of that variable identifier within the activation denotes that variable.

(g) A *reference* for each variable identifier that is a formal variable parameter identifier for the block; the reference is to the variable that is denoted by the corresponding actual parameter when the algorithm commences. Each occurrence of that variable identifier within the activation denotes the referenced variable.

(h) A *reference* to a procedure or function for each formal procedural or functional parameter identifier for the block; the reference is to the procedure or function that is denoted by the corresponding actual parameter when the algorithm commences. Each occurrence of that procedure identifier or function identifier within the activation denotes that procedure or function.

(i) If the activated block is a function block, a *result* that is undefined when the algorithm commences.

An activation of the block of a procedure or function is said to be *within* the activation that contains the procedure or function. If an activation A is within an activation B, then A is also said to be *within* any other activation that B is within.

A procedure statement or function designator that is contained in an algorithm and that specifies the activation of a block is called the *activation-point* of that activation.

11.   Procedures and Functions

Procedures and functions are named program parts that are activated by procedure statements (Section 9.1.2) and function designators (Section 8.1), respectively. The programmer can declare new procedures and functions as needed. Procedure declarations and function declarations are collected into procedure and function declaration parts.

> *ProcedureAndFunctionDeclarationPart* =
>   { (*ProcedureDeclaration* | *FunctionDeclaration*) ";" } .

In addition, each implementation is required to provide numerous "predeclared" procedures and functions. Since these, as all such entities, are assumed to be declared in a scope surrounding the program, no conflict arises from a declaration redefining the same identifier within the program.

11.1.   Procedure Declarations

A procedure declaration serves to introduce a procedure identifier, and to associate the identifier with a block and possibly with a formal parameter list. The procedure heading of a procedure declaration introduces the procedure identifier and the formal parameter list.

A procedure may be declared by a single procedure declaration consisting of the procedure heading and the block. This is the most common form.

Alternatively, it may be declared with a "forward declaration": one procedure declaration consists of the procedure heading and the directive forward, and a second declaration in the same procedure and function declaration part consists of a procedure identification and the block. The procedure identifier in the procedure identification must be the identifier introduced by the first declaration. Note that the formal parameter list, if any, is not specified in the second declaration.

> *ProcedureDeclaration* =   *ProcedureHeading* ";" *Block* |
>   *ProcedureHeading* ";" *Directive* |
>   *ProcedureIdentification* ";" *Block* .
>
> *ProcedureHeading* = "procedure" *Identifier* [*FormalParameterList*] .
>
> *ProcedureIdentification* = "procedure" *ProcedureIdentifier* .
>
> *ProcedureIdentifier* = *Identifier* .

The use of the procedure identifier in a procedure statement within the block of its declaration implies recursive execution of the procedure.

Example of procedure and function declaration part containing procedures:

```
procedure ReadInteger (var F: Text;  var X: Integer);
    var S: Natural;
begin
    while F↑ <> ' ' do Get(F);
    S := 0;
    while F↑ in ['0'..'9'] do
        begin
        S := 10 * S + (ord(F↑)-ord('0'));
        Get(F)
        end;
    X := S
end { ReadInteger } ;

procedure Bisect(function F(X: Real): Real; A, B: Real; var Z: Real);
    var M: Real;
begin
    { assume F(A) < 0 and F(B) > 0 }
    while abs(A-N) > 1e-10 * abs(A) do
        begin
        M := (A + B) / 2.0;
        if F(M) < 0 then  A := M  else  B := M
        end;
    Z := M
end { Bisect } ;

procedure GCD(M, N: Integer;  var X, Y, Z: Integer);
    { Greatest Common Divisor X of M and N, assuming M>=0 and N>0. }
    { Extended Euclid's Algorithm }
    var A1, A2, B1, B2, C, D, Q, R: Integer;
begin
    A1 := 0;  A2 := 1;  B1 := 1;  B2 := 0;  C := M;  D := N;
    while D <> 0 do
        begin
        {A1*M + B1*N = D, A2*M + B2*N = C, and GCD(C,D) = GCD(M,N)}
        Q := C div R;  R := C mod D;
        A2 := A2 - Q*A1;  B2 := B2 - Q*B1;
        C := D;  D := R;
        R := A1;  A1 := A2;  A2 := R;
        R := B1;  B1 := B2;  B2 := R
        end;
    X := C;  Y := A2;  Z := B2
    { X = GCD(M,N) = Y*M + Z*N }
end { GCD };
```

11.2 Function Declarations

A function declaration serves to introduce a function identifier, and to associate the identifier with a result type, with a block, and possibly with a formal parameter list. The function heading of a function declaration introduces the function identifier, the result type, and the formal parameter list.

A function may be declared by a single function declaration consisting of the function heading and the block. This is the most common form.

Alternatively, it may be declared with a "forward declaration": one function declaration consists of the function heading and the directive forward, and a second declaration in the same procedure and function declaration part consists of a function identification and the block. The function identifier in the function identification must be the identifier introduced by the first declaration. Note that the formal parameter list, if any, and the result type are not specified in the second declaration.

FunctionDeclaration = *FunctionHeading* ";" *Block* |
  FunctionHeading ";" *Directive* |
  FunctionIdentification ";" *Block* .

FunctionHeading =
  "function" *Identifier* [*FormalParameterList*] ":" *ResultType* .

ResultType =
  OrdinalTypeIdentifier | *RealTypeIdentifier* | *PointerTypeIdentifier* .

FunctionIdentification = "function" *FunctonIdentifier* .
FunctionIdentifier = *Identifier* .

The block of a function declaration must contain at least one assignment statement that assigns to the function identifier. The use of the function identifier in a function designator within the block of its declaration implies recursive execution of the function.

Example of procedure and function declaration part containing functions:
```
function sqrt(X: Real): Real;
    { Newton's method }
    var X0, X1: Real;
begin
    X1 := X;  { X > 1, Newton's method }
    repeat  X0 := X1;   X1 := (X0 + X/X0)*0.5
    until abs(X1 - X0) < Eps * X1;
    sqrt := X0
end { sqrt } ;
```

```
function Max(A: Vector;   N: Integer): Real;
   { Return the maximum value of elements A[1], ..., A[N]. }
   var X: Real;   I: Integer;
begin
   X := A[1];
   for I := 2 to N do
      begin  { X = Max( A[1], ..., A[I-1] ) }
         if X < A[I] then X := A[I]
      end;
   { X = Max( A[1], ..., A[N] ) }
   Max := X
end { Max } ;

function GCD(M, N: Natural): Natural;
begin if N = 0 then GCD := M else GCD := GCD(N, M mod N) end;

function Power(X: Real;   Y: Natural): Real;
   var W, Z: Real;   I: Natural;
begin
   W := X;   Z := 1;   I := Y;
   while I > 0 do
      begin
         { Z * (W ** I) = X ** Y }
         if odd(I) then Z := Z * W;
         I := I div 2;
         W := sqr(W)
      end;
   { Z = X ** Y }
   Power := Z
end { Power } ;
```

11.3 Parameters

Parameters allow each activation of a procedure or function to operate on entities (values, variables, procedures, and functions) that are specified at the activation point (see Section 10.3) by an actual parameter list. The formal parameter list in the procedure or function heading determines the identifiers by which those entities are known in the block of the procedure or function, and the nature and type required of the actual parameters.

The actual parameters for predeclared procedures and functions do not always conform to the rules for ordinary procedures and functions (see Sections 11.4, 11.5 and 12).

11.3.1. Formal parameter lists.

> *FormalParameterList* =   "(" *FormalParameterSection*
>   { ";" *FormalParameterSection* } ")" .
>
> *FormalParameterSection*= *ValueParameterSpecification* |
>   *VariableParameterSpecification* |
>   *ProceduralParameterSpecification* |
>   *FunctionalParameterSpecification* .

The parameters specified by a formal parameter section are either value, variable, procedural, or functional parameters.

11.3.1.1. Formal value and variable parameters.

A value or variable parameter specification introduces each of the identifiers in its identifier list as a variable identifier. If a type identifier occurs, it denotes the type possessed by each variable identifier. If a conformant array schema occurs, each of the variable identifiers is called a conformant array parameter, and the type that it possesses depends on the type of the actual parameter. Within a given activation, all formal parameters defined in the same formal parameter section possess the same type.

Note: Conformant array schemas may not be supported by all implementations of Pascal. In particular, Level 0 implementations do not support them, whereas Level 1 implementations do.

> *ValueParameterSpecification* =
>   *IdentifierList* ":" (*TypeIdentifier* |
>   *ConformantArraySchema*).
>
> *VariableParameterSpecification* =
>   "var" *IdentifierList* ":" (*TypeIdentifier* |
>   *ConformantArraySchema*) .
>
> *ConformantArraySchema* =   *PackedConformantArraySchema* |
>   *UnpackedConformantArraySchema* .
>
> *PackedConformantArraySchema* =
>   "packed" "array" "[" *IndexTypeSpecification* "]" "of" *TypeIdentifier* .
>
> *UnpackedConformantArraySchema* =
>   "array" "[" *IndexTypeSpecification* { ";" *IndexTypeSpecification* } "]"
>   "of" (*TypeIdentifier* | *ConformantArraySchema*) .
>
> *IndexTypeSpecification* =   *Identifier* ".." *Identifier* ":"
>   *OrdinalTypeIdentifier* .
>
> *BoundIdentifier* = *Identifier* .

An index type specification introduces the two identifiers as bound identifiers possessing the type denoted by the ordinal type identifier. The conformant array schema

```
array [Low1..High1: T1; Low2..High2: T2] of T
```

is simply an abbreviation for

```
array [Low1..High1: T1] of array [Low2..High2: T2] of T.
```

Example of a function declaration illustrating conformant array parameter:
```
{This example is derived from the function Max shown in 11.2. }
function Max (A: array [L..H: Integer] of Real;  N: Integer): Real;
   { Return the maximum value of elements A[L],...,A[N]. }
   var X: Real;  I: Integer;
begin
   X:= A[L];
   for I := succ(L) to N do
      begin  { X = Max( A[L],...,A[I-1] ) }
         if X < A[I] then X := A[I]
      end;
   { X = Max( A[L],...,A[N] ) }
   Max := X
end { Max } ;
```

11.3.1.2. Formal procedural and functional parameters. A procedural parameter specification introduces the procedure identifier with any associated formal parameter list defined by the procedure heading.

ProceduralParameterSpecification = ProcedureHeading .

A functional parameter specification introduces the function identifier with the result type and any associated formal parameter list defined by the function heading

FunctionalParameterSpecification = FunctionHeading.

11.3.2. Actual parameter lists. An actual parameter list at an activation point, i.e., at a procedure statement or a function designator, specifies the actual parameters that are to be substituted for the formal parameters of the procedure or function for that activation. If the procedure or function has no formal parameter list, then there must be no actual parameter list. The correspondence between actual

parameters and formal parameters is established by positions of the parameters in their respective lists. The order of substitution of actual parameters in a list is implementation-dependent.

> *ActualParameterList* = `"("` *Actual Parameter* { `","`
> *ActualParameter* } `")"` .
>
> *ActualParameter*   = *Expression* | *Variable* |
> *ProcedureIdentifier* | *FunctionIdentifier* .

All actual parameters at a given activation point that correspond to formal conformant array parameters defined in the same formal parameter section must possess the same type, which must be conformable (Section 11.3.4) with the conformant array schema of the formal parameter section. All of the corresponding formal parameters within a given activation have the same type, which is derived through the conformant array schema from the type of the actual parameter(s) (see Section 11.3.4).

11.3.2.1. Actual value parameters. An actual value parameter is an expression. The formal parameter denotes a variable that is assigned the value of the actual parameter when the variable is created (see Section 10.3).

If the formal parameter is not a conformant array parameter, then the value of the actual parameter must be assignment-compatible (see Section 6.5) with the type of the formal parameter.

If the formal parameter is a conformant array parameter, then the type of the actual parameter must not be a conformant type (see Section 11.3.4).

11.3.2.2. Actual variable parameters. An actual variable parameter is a variable. Throughout the activation the formal parameter denotes the variable that is denoted by the actual parameter when the activation commences (see Section 10.3). The actual parameter must denote neither a component of a packed array or record variable nor a tag field.

If the formal parameter is not a conformant array parameter, then the actual parameter and the formal parameter must possess the same type.

11.3.2.3. Actual procedural parameters. An actual procedural parameter is a procedure identifier. The formal parameter denotes the procedure that is denoted by the actual parameter (see Section 10.3).

The formal parameter lists, if any, of the formal and actual parameters must be congruent (Section 11.3.3).

11.3.2.4. Actual functional Parameters. An actual functional parameter is a function identifier. The formal parameter denotes the function that is denoted by the actual parameter (see Section 10.3). The result types of the formal and actual parameters must denote the same type. The formal parameter lists, if any, of the formal and actual parameters must be congruent (Section 11.3.3).

11.3.3. Parameter-list congruity. Two formal parameter lists are *congruent* if they have the same number of parameter sections, and if corresponding formal parameter sections satisfy one of the following conditions.

(a)   Both are value parameter specifications with the same number of identifiers in their identifier lists, and either they both contain type identifiers that denote the same type or else they both contain equivalent conformant array schemas.

(b)   Both are variable parameter specifications with the same number of identifiers in their identifier lists, and either they both contain type identifiers that denote the same type or else they both contain equivalent conformant array schemas.

(c)   Both are procedural parameter specifications with congruent formal parameter lists.

(d)   Both are functional parameter specifications with congruent formal parameter lists and with result types that denote the same type.

Two conformant array schemas (each with a single index type specification) are *equivalent* if all three of the following conditions are true.

(a)   The ordinal type identifiers in the index type specifications denote the same type.

(b)   Either each contains a component conformant array schema and the component schemas are equivalent, or else each contains a component type identifier and the component type identifiers denote the same type.

(c)   Both schemas are packed conformant array schemas or else both are unpacked conformant array schemas.

Example of two equivalent conformant array schemas:
```
array [L1..H1: Integer; L2..H2: Color] of
                           packed array [L3..H3: T2] of T

array [Low1..High1: Integer] of array [Low2..High2: Color] of
                           packed array [Low3..High3: T2] of T
```

11.3.4. Conformability and conformant types. An array type T (with a single index type) is said to be *conformable* with a conformant array schema S (with a single index type specification) if all of the following conditions are true. Let I represent the ordinal type identifier of the index type specification of S.

(a)   The index type of T is compatible with the type denoted by I.

(b)   Every value of the index type of T is a member of the set of values of the type denoted by I.

(c)   If S does not contain a conformant array schema, then the component type of T is the same as the type denoted by the type identifier in S; otherwise, the component type of T is conformable with the component schema of S.

(d)   T is packed if and only if S is a packed conformant array schema.

Wherever conformability is required, it is an error if condition (b) does not hold.

A type that is called a *conformant type derived through* S *from* T is an array type that has the same index type as T, is packed if and only if T is packed, and has a component type that either is the same type as the component type of T or else, if S contains another component conformant array schema, is a conformant type derived through the component schema from the component type of T. The bound identifiers introduced in the index type specification denote the smallest and largest values of the index type of the conformant type.

11.4. Predeclared Procedures

11.4.1. File handling procedures. There are several predeclared procedures that are specifically defined for use with textfiles. These are described in detail in Section 12. The following procedures operate on any file variable f (see Sections 6.2.4 and 7.4).

Rewrite(f) causes f to have an empty sequence and to be in generation mode.

Put(f) is an error if f is undefined or is not in generation mode, or if the buffer variable f↑ is undefined. Appends the value of f↑ to the end of the sequence of f.

Reset(f) causes f to be placed in inspection mode, and the position in its sequence becomes the first position. If the sequence is empty, eof(f) becomes true and f↑ becomes totally undefined; otherwise, eof(f) becomes false and f↑ takes on the value of the first component of the sequence.

Get(f) is an error if f is undefined or if eof(f) is true. Causes the position in the sequence to be advanced to the next component, if any, and f↑ to take on its value; if no next component exists, eof(f) becomes true and f↑ becomes totally undefined.

In each of the following definitions, all occurrences of f denote the same file variable, the symbols v,v1,...,vn represent variables, and e,e1,...,en represent expressions. Note that the variables v,v1,..., and vn are not actual variable parameters, and thus they may be components of packed arrays or records.

Read(f,v1,...,vn) is equivalent to the statement

begin Read(f,v1);...;Read(f,vn) end

Read(f,v) where f is not a textfile is equivalent to the statement

begin v:= f↑; Get(f) end

Write(f,e1,...,en) is equivalent to the statement

begin Write(f,e1);...;Write(f,en) end

Write(f,e) where f is not a textfile is equivalent to the statement

begin f↑ := e; Put(f) end

11.4.2. Dynamic allocation procedures. Dynamic allocation procedures are the means by which new pointer values and their identified variables are created (New) and destroyed (Dispose). In these descriptions, p is a pointer variable, q is a pointer expression, and c1,...,cn, k1,...,kn are constants. Note that p is not an actual variable parameter, and thus it may be a component of a packed array or record.

New(p)

creates a new identifying pointer value having the type that is possessed by p and assigns it to p. The identified variable p↑ is totally undefined.

New(p,c1,...,cn)

creates a new identifying pointer value having the type that is possessed by p and assigns it to p. The identified variable p↑ is totally undefined. The domain type of that pointer type must be a record type with variant part. The first constant (c1) selects a variant from the variant part; the next constant, if any, selects a variant from the next (nested) variant part, and so on. It is an error if any other variants in those variant parts except the selected ones are made active in the identified variable. It is an error if the identified variable p↑ is used as a factor, as an actual variable parameter, or as the variable in an assignment statement (although components of p↑ may occur in those contexts).

Dispose(q)

destroys the identifying value q. It is an error if q is nil. The value q must have been created by the first (short) form of New, otherwise it is an error.

Dispose(q,k1,...,kn)

destroys the identifying value q. It is an error if q is nil. The value q must have been created by the second (long) form of New and the constants k1,...,kn must select the same variants that were selected when the value was created, otherwise it is an error.

11.4.3.   Data transfer procedures. Let U denote an unpacked array variable having type S1 as its index type and T as its component type. Let P denote a packed array variable having S2 as its index type and T as its component type. Let B and C denote the smallest and largest values of type S2. Let K denote a new variable (not otherwise accessible) possessing type S1 and let J denote a new variable possessing type S2. Let I be an expression that is compatible with S1.

Pack(U,I,P) is equivalent to the statement

```
begin
   K := I;
   for J := B to C do
      begin
         P[J] := U[K];
         if J <> C then K := succ(K)
      end
end
```

Unpack(P,U,I) is equivalent to the statement

```
begin
   K := I;
   for J := B to C do
      begin
         U[K] := P[J];
         if J <> C then K := succ(K)
      end
end
```

In each equivalence, P denotes one variable and U denotes one variable during all iterations of the for statement.

11.5. Predeclared Functions

11.5.1. Arithmetic functions. Let x be any real or integer expression. The result type of abs and sqr is the same as the type of x. The result type of the other arithmetic functions is real.

abs(x)   yields the absolute value of x.

sqr(x)   yields the square of x. It is an error if the square does not exist in the implementation.

sin(x)   yields the sine of x, where x is in radians.

cos(x)   yields the cosine of x, where x is in radians.

exp(x)   yields the value of the base of natural logarithms raised to the power x.

ln(x)   yields the natural logarithm of x. It is an error if x is less than or equal to zero.

sqrt(x)   yields the square root of x. It is an error if x is negative.

arctan(x) yields the principal value, in radians, of the arctangent of x.

11.5.2. Boolean functions. Let i be any integer expression, and let f denote any file variable. The result type of each Boolean function is Boolean.

odd(i)   is equivalent to the expression (abs(i) mod 2 = 1).

eof(f)   is an error if f is undefined; otherwise, eof(f) yields true if f is in generation mode or if f is positioned past the last component in its sequence. If the parameter list is omitted, eof is applied to the program parameter Input.

eoln(f)   is an error if f is undefined or if eof(f) is true. f must be a textfile. Eoln(f) yields true if the current component of the sequence of f is an end-of-line marker. If the parameter list is omitted, eoln is applied to the program parameter Input.

11.5.3. Transfer functions. Let r denote a real expression. The result type of these functions is Integer.

trunc(r)   yields a value such that if r >= 0 then 0 <= r – trunc(r) < 1, and if r < 0 then –1 < r – trunc(r) <= 0. It is an error if no such value exists.

round(r)   yields a value such that if r >= 0 then round(r) = trunc(r + 0.5), and if r < 0 then round(r) = trunc(r – 0.5). It is an error if no such value exists.

11.5.4 Ordinal functions. Let i be an integer expression, and let x be any ordinal expression.

ord(x)   yields the ordinal number of x.

chr(i)   yields the value of type Char having ordinal number i. It is an error if no such value exists. If c denotes a character value then chr(ord(c)) = c is always true.

succ(x)   yields the successor of x, if any exists, in which case ord(succ(x)) = ord(x) + 1. It is an error if no successor exists.

pred(x)   yields the predecessor of x, if any exists, in which case ord(pred(x)) = ord(x) - 1. It is an error if no predecessor exists.

12. Textfile Input and Output

The basis for legible input and output are textfiles (see Section 6.2.4) that are passed as program parameters (see Section 13) to a Pascal program and that in the program's environment may represent some input or output devices such as a keyboard, display, a magnetic tape, or a line printer. In order to facilitate the handling of textfiles, three predeclared procedures (Readln, Writeln, and Page) are introduced, and two predeclared procedures (Read and Write — see Section 11.4.1) are extended. The textfiles that these procedures apply to need not represent input or output devices, but can also be local files. The actual parameter lists for these procedures do not conform to the usual rules (Section 11.3), allowing among other things for a variable number of parameters. Moreover, the parameters need not be of type Char, but also may be of certain other types, in which case the data transfer is accompanied by an implicit data conversion operation. If the first parameter is a file variable, then this is the file to be read or written. Otherwise, the program parameters Input and Output (see Section 13) are assumed for reading and writing, respectively.

12.1 Read

When using Read on a textfile, the following rules apply. Let f denote a textfile, and let v1,...,vn denote variables possessing type Char or Integer (or subrange of either) or Real.

(a)   Read(v1,...,vn) is equivalent of Read(g,v1,...,vn), where g denotes the textfile program parameter Input.

(b)   Read(f,v1,...,vn) is equivalent to the statement

        begin Read(f,v1);...;Read(f,vn) end

where all occurrences of f denote a single variable.

(c)   Read(f,v) is an error if f is undefined or if f in not in inspection mode or if eof(f) is true.

The effect of Read(f,v) depends on the type of v.

12.1.1.   Char Read. Read(f,v), where v denotes a variable possessing a type that is compatible with type Char, is equivalent to the statement

        begin   v := f↑; Get(f)   end

where all occurrences of f denote a single variable. If eoln(f) is true before Read(f,v), then (v = ' ') will be true after.

12.1.2.   Integer Read. Read(f,v), where v denotes a variable possessing a type that is compatible with type Integer, implies the reading from f of a sequence of characters which form a *SignedInteger* (see Section 4) and the assignment of the integer value denoted thereby to v. The value must be assignment-compatible with the type of v. Preceding spaces and end-of-line markers are skipped. It is an error if the signed integer is not found.

12.1.3.   Real Read. Read(f,v), where v denotes a variable possessing the type Real, implies the reading from f of a sequence of characters which form a *SignedNumber* (see Section 4) and the assignment of the real value denoted thereby to v. Preceding spaces and end-of-line markers are skipped. It is an error if the signed number is not found.

12.2   Readln

Let f denote a textfile, and let v1,...,vn denote variables of type Char or Integer (or subrange of either), or Real.

       Readln(v1,...,vn) is equivalent to Readln(g,v1,...,vn), and Readln is equivalent to Readln(g), where g denotes the textfile program parameter Input.

Readln(f,v1,...,vn) is equivalent to the statement

```
begin  Read(f,v1,...,vn); Readln(f)  end
```

where all occurrences of f denote a single variable.

Readln(f) is equivalent to the statement

```
begin
   while not eoln(f) do Get(f);
   Get(f)
end
```

where all occurrences of f denote a single variable.

12.3. Write

When using Write on a textfile, the following rules apply. Let f denote a textfile, p,p1,...,pn denote *WriteParameters,* e denote an expression, and m and n denote integer expressions. The actual parameter list for write must have the following syntax.

> *WriteParameterList* =   "(" (*FileVariable* | *WriteParameter*)
>   { "," *WriteParameter* } ")" .
>
> *WriteParameter* = *Expression* [":" *IntegerExpression*
>   [":" *IntegerExpression*]] .

(a) Write(p1,...,pn) is equivalent to Write(g,p1,...,pn), where g denotes the textfile program parameter Output.

(b) Write(f,p1,...,pn) is equivalent to the statement

```
begin  Write(f,p1);...;Write(f,pn) end
```

where all occurrences of f denote a single variable.

(c) Write(f,p) is an error if f is undefined or not in generation mode.

(d) Each write parameter has one of the following forms:

```
e      e:m     e:m:n
```

e represents the value to be "written" on f, and m and n are so-called field-width parameters. It is an error if either m or n is less than or equal to zero. The type of e must be either Integer, Real, Char, Boolean, or a string type. The expression n may occur only if e is of type Real (see Section 12.3.3). If m is omitted, a default value is assumed. The default value is implementation-defined if e is of type Integer, Real, or Boolean. The default value for type Char is 1, and the default value for a string type is the number of components in the string.

   If the representation of the value of e requires fewer than m characters, then it is preceded by an adequate number of spaces so that exactly m characters are written.

The representation of the value of e depends on the type of e.

12.3.1.   Char Write.   If e is of type Char, then Write(f,e:m) is equivalent to the statement

```
begin
   for J := 1 to m - 1 do Write(f,' ');
   f↑ := e; Put(f)
end
```

where all occurrences of f denote a single variable, and where J denotes a new (not otherwise accessible) integer variable.

12.3.2.   Integer Write.   If e is of type Integer, then Write(f,e:m) writes a '-' if e < 0, followed by the decimal representation of abs(e). Preceding spaces are written if needed to write m characters.

12.3.3.   Real Write.   If e is of type Real, Write(f,e:m:n) writes a fixed-point representation with n digits after the decimal point; and Write (f,e:m) writes a floating-point representation. The operator "**" means "raised to the power."

12.3.3.1.   Fixed-point representation.   Let w be zero if e is zero, otherwise let w be the absolute value of e rounded and then truncated to n decimal places. Let d be 1 if w < 1, otherwise let $10^{**}(d-1) <= w < 10^{**}d$. d is the number of digits to the left of the decimal point. Let s = ord((e < 0) and (w <> 0)). The representation is negative if s = 1. Let k = (s + d + 1 + n); k is the number of non-blank characters written.

   If k < m, then m-k preceding spaces are written. The fixed-point representation of e consists of k characters:

(a)   '-' if s = 1,

(b)   the d decimal digits of the integer part of w,

(c)   '.',

(d)   the n most significant decimal digits of the
fractional part of w.

12.3.3.2. Floating-point representation. The number of digits that
are to occur in the scale factor ("E part") of the floating-point representation is implementation-defined; let x denote this number. Let k
be the larger of m and x+6. The number of significant digits to be
written is k-x-4, with one digit before the decimal point and d digits
after (thus d = k-x-5). Let w and s be zero if e is zero. If e is nonzero,
then let s be such that 10.0**s <= abs(e) < 10.0**(s+1), and let w be
(abs(e)/10.0**s) + 0.5 * 10.0**(-d). If w >= 10.0 then w and s must be
adjusted by s := s + 1 and w := w / 10.0. Finally, w is truncated to d
decimal places.

The floating-point representation of e consists of:

(a)   either '-' if ((e < 0) and (w <> 0)) or else ' ',

(b)   the most significant decimal digit of w,

(c)   '.',

(d)   the d next-most-significant decimal digits of w,

(e)   either 'e' or 'E' (the choice being implementation-defined),

(f)   '-' if s < 0, otherwise '+',

(g)   x decimal digits of s with leading zeros if needed.

12.3.4. Boolean Write. If e is of type Boolean, then a representation
of the words true or false is written by the statement Write(f,e:m),
which is equivalent to the statement

```
if e then Write(f,'true':m) else Write(f,'false':m)
```

with the exception that the case of the letters written is implementation-
defined.

12.3.5. String Write. If e possesses a string type of length k, then
Write(f,e:m) writes m - k spaces if m > k, followed by the components

of e having successive indices starting at 1 and ascending to either k or m, whichever is less.

12.4. Writeln

Let f denote a textfile, and let p1,...,pn denote write parameters.

Writeln(p1,...,pn) is equivalent to Writeln(g,p1,...,pn), and Writeln is equivalent to Writeln(g), where g denotes the textfile program parameter Output.

Writeln(f,p1,...,pn) is equivalent to the statement

```
begin Write(f,p1,...,pn); Writeln(f) end
```

where all occurrences of f denote a single variable.

Writeln(f) appends an end-of-line marker to the sequence of file f. It is an error if f is undefined or if f is not in generaton mode.

12.5. Page

Page(f) implies an implementation-defined effect on the textfile f, such that any text subsequently written to f will appear at the top of a new page when f is printed. If f is not empty, and the last component of its sequence is not an end-of-line marker, then Page(f) performs an implicit Writeln(f). If the parameter list is omitted, the textfile program parameter Output is assumed. It is an error if f is undefined or if f is not in generation mode.

The effect of reading a file variable to which Page was previously applied is implementation-dependent.

13. Programs

A Pascal program consists of a program heading and a block.

Program = ProgramHeading ";" *Block* "." .

ProgramHeading = "program" *Identifier* [*ProgramParameterList*] .

ProgramParameterList = "(" *IdentifierList* ")" .

The identifier following the symbol program is the program name; it has no further significance inside the program. Each identifier in the program parameter list is called a program parameter, and denotes an entity that exists outside the program and that, therefore, is called *external*. It is through its program parameters that the program communicates with its environment.

When a program is activated, each program parameter is bound to the external entity that it represents. For those program parameters that are file variables, the binding is implementation-defined; for all other program parameters, the binding is implementation-dependent.

Each program parameter, with the exception of Input and Output, must be declared in the variable declaration part of the program's block. In the case of Input or Output, the occurrence of the identifier in the program parameter list has the effect of implicitly declaring the identifier to be a textfile in the program block, and implicitly performing a Reset(Input) or Rewrite(Output) at the commencement of each activation of the program.

The effect of applying Reset or Rewrite to either Input or Output is implementation-defined.

Examples of programs:
```
program CopyReals(F,G);
    var F, G: file of Real; R: Real;
begin
    Reset(F); Rewrite(G);
    while not eof(F) do
        begin  Read(F,R); Write(G,R)  end
end { CopyReals } .


program CopyText(Input,Output);
begin
    while not eof(Input) do
        begin
            while not eoln(Input) do
                begin Input↑ := Output↑; Put(Output); Get(Input) end;
            Readln(Input); Writeln(Output)
        end
end { CopyText } .
```

14. Compliance with ISO 7185

A *program* complies with the ISO Pascal standard [see Reference 11] if it uses only the features of the language that are defined by the standard and it does not rely on any particular interpretation of implementation-dependent features. The program is said to comply at level 0 if it does not make use of comformant array parameters, or at level 1 if it does.

A *processor* is defined by the standard to be "a system or mechanism that accepts a program as input, prepares it for execution, and executes the process so defined with data to produce results." A processor complies with the standard if it satisfies all of the following conditions.

(a) It accepts all features of the language as they are defined by the standard. It is said to comply at level 0 if it does not accept conformant array parameters, or at level 1 if it does.

(b) It does not require the use of substitute or additional language elements in order to accomplish a feature of the language.

(c) It is able to recognize violations of the standard that are not specifically called errors, and reports such violations to the user. If the processor does not examine all of the program for violations, then it must report this fact as well.

(d) It handles each violation that is specifically called an error in one of the following ways.
    1. It states in its documentation that the error is not reported.

    2. It reports during program preparation that the error is possible.

    3. It reports during program preparation that the error will occur.

    4. It reports during program execution that the error occurred.

(e) It is able to process as an error any use of an extension or of an implementation-dependent feature.

(f) It is accompanied by a document that contains the following.
    1. A definition of all implementation-defined features.

    2. A section that describes all errors that are not reported (see d.1, above). If an extension makes use of a condition that is specified by the standard to be an error and thus the error is not reported, then the document must state that the error is not reported.

    3. A section that describes all extensions supported by the implementation.

References

1. N. Wirth, "The Programming Language Pascal", *Acta Informatica*, 1, 35-63, 1971.

2. N. Wirth, "Program Development by Stepwise Refinement", *Communications of the ACM 14*, 221-227, April 1971.

3. N. Wirth, *Systematic Programming*, Prentice-Hall, Inc. 1973.

4. O.J. Dahl, E.W. Dijkstra, C.A.R. Hoare, *Structured Programming*, Academic Press Inc. 1972.

5. C.A.R. Hoare and N. Wirth, "An Axiomatic Definition of the Programming Language Pascal", *Acta Informatica*, 2, 335-355, 1973.

6. D.E. Knuth, The Art of Computer Programming, vol 1, *Fundamental Algorithms*, Addison-Wesley, 1968.

7. N. Wirth, "An Assessment of the Programming Language Pascal", SIG-PLAN Notices, *10*, 23-30, June 1975.

8. N. Wirth, "The Design of a Pascal Compiler", *SOFTWARE —Practice and Experience, 1*, 309-333, 1971.

9. N. Wirth, *Algorithms + Data Structures = Programs*, Prentice Hall, Inc., 1976.

10. D. Barron, "A Perspective on Pascal" and J. Welsh, W. Sneeringer, and C.A.R. Hoare, "Ambiguities and Insecurities in Pascal" *Pascal—The Language and its Implementation,* John Wiley, 1981.

11. International Organization for Standardization, *Specification for Computer Programming Language Pascal,* ISO 7185-1982, 1982.

12. A.H.J. Sale and B. Wichmann "The Pascal Validation Suite", *Pascal News 16,* 5-153, 1979.

13. N. Wirth, "What Can We Do About the Unnecessary Diversity of Notation for Syntactic Definitions?" *Communications of the ACM 20,* 822-823, November, 1977.

14. B. Wichmann and Z.J. Ciechanowicz *Pascal Compiler Validation,* John Wiley, 1983.

APPENDIX A

Predeclared Procedures and Functions

Abs(x)

an arithmetic function that computes the real absolute value of a real
parameter x or the integer absolute value of an integer parameter x.

ArcTan(x)

an arithmetic function that computes the real arctangent (principal value)
in radians of a real or integer parameter x.

Chr(i)

a transfer function that returns the character whose ordinal number is the
integer parameter i. Chr(i) is an error if such a character value does not exist.

Dispose(q)

a dynamic-allocation procedure that deallocates an identified variable q↑
and destroys the identifying value q. Dispose(q) is an error if q is nil or
undefined. The value q must have been created by the short form of New.

Dispose(q,k1,...,kn)

a dynamic-allocation procedure that deallocates an identified record variable q↑ and destroys the identifying value q. Dispose(q,k1,...,kn) is an error if
q is nil or undefined. The value q must have been created by the long form of
New and k1,...,kn must select the same variants selected when q was created.

Eof(f)

a Boolean function that returns true if the file variable f if f is in
generation mode, or if f is positioned past the last component in its sequence
and f is in inspection mode. eof(f) is an error if f is undefined. Otherwise
eof(f) returns false. If f is omitted, program parameter Input is assumed.

Eoln(f)

a Boolean function that returns true if the textfile f, when in inspection
mode, is positioned at an end-of-line marker. eoln(f) is an error if f is

204

undefined or if eof(f) is true. Otherwise eoln(f) returns false. If f is omitted, program parameter Input is assumed.

Exp(x)

an arithmetic function that computes the real value of e (the base of natural logarithms) raised to the real or integer parameter x.

Get(f)

a file-handling procedure that causes the position in the sequence f to be advanced to the next component, if any, and f↑ to take on its value; if no next component exists eof(f) becomes true and f↑ becomes totally undefined. Get(f) is an error if f is undefined or eof(f) is true. If f is omitted, program parameter Input is assumed.

Ln(x)

an arithmetic function that computes the real natural logarithm (to the base e) of the real or integer parameter x, where x > 0. Ln(x) is an error if x<=0.

New(p)

a dynamic-allocation procedure that allocates a new identified (dynamic) variable p↑ having the domain type of p and creates a new identifying pointer value having the type possessed by p and assigns it to p. If p↑ is a variant record, New(p) allocates enough space to accommodate all variants.

New(p,c1,...,cn)

a dynamic-allocation procedure that allocates a new identified (dynamic) variable p↑ having the variant record type of p with tagfield values c1,...,cn for n nested variant parts, and creates a new identifying pointer value having the type possessed by p and assigns it to p.

Odd(i)

a Boolean function that returns true if the integer parameter i is not evenly divisible by 2; returns false otherwise.

Ord(x)

a transfer function that returns the ordinal number (an integer) of the ordinal parameter x in the set of values defined by the type of x.

Pack(u,i,p)

a data-transfer procedure that packs the contents of the unpacked array u starting at component i into the packed array p.

Page(f)

a file-handling procedure that causes an implementation-defined effect on the textfile parameter f such that any text subsequently written to f will appear at the top of a new page when f is printed. If f is not empty, and the last component of its sequence is not an end-of-line marker, then Page(f) performs an implicit Writeln(f). If the parameter list is omitted, the textfile program parameter Output is assumed. Page(f) is an error if f is undefined or if f is not in generation mode.

Pred(x)
a ordinal function that returns the previous ordinal value (predecessor) before the ordinal parameter x, if a predecessor exists: ord(pred(x)) = ord(x) − 1. Pred(x) is an error if x is the smallest value of its type.

Put(f)
a file-handling procedure that appends the value of f↑ to the end of the sequence of f. Put(f) is an error if f is undefined or is not in generation mode or if the buffer variable f↑ is undefined. Following Put(f), f↑ is totally undefined.

Read(f,v)
See User Manual, Chapters 9 and 12, and Report Sections 11.4 and 12.1.

Read(f,v1,...,vn)
See User Manual, Chapters 9 and 12, and Report Sections 11.4 and 12.1.

Readln
See User Manual, Chapters 9 and 12, and Report Section 12.2.

Readln(f,v1,...,vn)
See User Manual, Chapters 9 and 12, and Report Section 12.2.

Reset(f)
a file-handling procedure that places f in inspection mode and causes the position of f to become the first position. If f is empty, eof(f) becomes true and f↑ becomes totally undefined. Otherwise eof(f) becomes false and f↑ becomes the value of the first component of the sequence.

Rewrite(f)
a file-handling procedure that replaces f with the empty sequence and places f in generation mode. Eof(f) becomes true.

Round(r)
a transfer function that computes trunc(r + 0.5) for the real parameter r >= 0.0, or trunc(r − 0.5) for the real parameter r < 0.0, if such a value exists in the type Integer. Otherwise it is an error.

Sin(x)
an arithmetic function that computes the real sine of a real or integer parameter x where x is in radians.

Sqr(x)

an arithmetic function that computes the real value x * x if x is real or the integer value x * x if x is integer. It is an error if that value does not exist.

Sqrt(x)

an arithmetic function that computes the real, non-negative square root of the integer or real parameter x where x >= 0. Sqrt(x) is an error if x < 0.

Succ(x)

an ordinal function that returns the next ordinal value (successor) after the ordinal parameter x, if such a successor exists: ord(succ(x)) = ord(x) + 1. succ(x) is an error if x is the largest value of ts type.

Trunc(r)

a transfer function that computes the greatest integer less than or equal to the real parameter r for r >= 0.0, or the least integer greater than or equal to the real parameter r, for r < 0.0 if such a value exists in the type Integer. Otherwise it is an error.

Unpack(p,u,i)

a data-transfer function that unpacks the packed array p into the unpacked array u starting at element i in the unpacked array.

Write(f,v)

See User Manual, Chapters 9 and 12, and Report Sections 11.4 and 12.3.

Write(f,v1,..,vn)

See User Manual, Chapters 9 and 12, and Report Sections 11.4 and 12.3.

Writeln

See User Manual, Chapters 9 and 12, and Report Section 12.4.

Writeln(f,e1,...,en)

See User Manual, Chapters 9 and 12, and Report Section 12.4.

APPENDIX B

Summary of Operators

Operator	Operation	Type of Operand	Result Type
Arithmetic			
+ (unary)	identity	integer or real	same as
– (unary)	sign inversion		operand
+	addition	integer or real	Integer
–	subtraction		or Real
*	multiplication		
div	integer division	integer	Integer
/	real division	integer or real	Real
mod	modulus	integer	Integer
Relational			
=	equality	simple, string,	Boolean
<>	inequality	set, or pointer	Boolean
<	less than	simple or string	Boolean
>	greater than		
<=	less or equal	simple or string	Boolean
	or set inclusion	set	
>=	greater or equal	simple or string	Boolean
	or set inclusion	set	
in	set membership	first operand is any ordinal base type, the second is its host set type	Boolean
Boolean			
not	negation	Boolean	Boolean
or	disjunction	"	"
and	conjunction	"	"

Set

+	union		
−	set difference	any set type T	T
*	intersection		

Operator Precedence in Expressions

Operator	*Classification*
not	logical negation
* / div mod and	multiplying operators
+ − or	adding operators
= <> > < >= <= in	relational operators

Other Operations

Notation	*Operation*	*Type of Operand*	*Result Type*
Assignment			
:=	assignment	Any assignable type	none
Variable Accessing			
[,]	array indexing	array	component type
.	field selection	record	field type
↑	identification	pointer	domain type
↑	buffer accessing	file	component type
Construction			
[,]	set construction	base type	set
' '	string construction	char	string

APPENDIX C

Tables

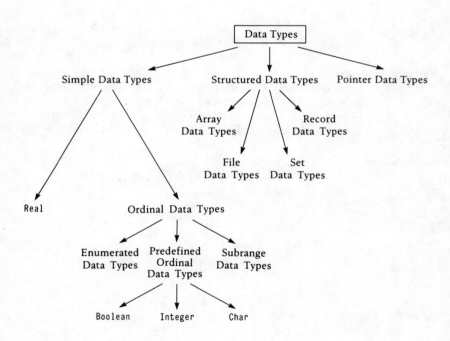

Figure C.a.   Complete Type Taxonomy of Data Types

Table of Standard Identifiers

Constants:

```
False, MaxInt, True
```

Types:

```
Boolean, Char, Integer, Real, Text
```

Variables:

```
Input, Output
```

Functions:

```
Abs, ArcTan, Chr, Cos, Eof, Eoln, Exp, Ln, Odd,
Ord, Pred, Round, Sin, Sqr, Sqrt, Succ, Trunc
```

Procedures:

```
Dispose, Get, New, Pack, Page, Put, Read, Readln,
Reset, Rewrite, Unpack, Write, Writeln
```

Alphabetical List:

Abs	False	Pack	Sin
ArcTan	Get	Page	Sqr
Boolean	Input	Pred	Sqrt
Char	Integer	Put	Succ
Chr	Ln	Read	Text
Cos	MaxInt	Readln	True
Dispose	New	Real	Trunc
Eof	Odd	Reset	Unpack
Eoln	Ord	Rewrite	Write
Exp	Output	Round	Writeln

Table of Symbols

Special Symbols:

```
+   -   *   /   =
<   >   <=  >=  <>
.   ,   :   ;   :=  ..
(   )   [   ]   ↑
```

Word Symbols (reserved words)

and	end	nil	set
array	file	not	then
begin	for	of	to

```
case       function    or          type
const      goto        packed      until
div        if          procedure   ver
do         in          program     while
downto     label       record      with
else       mod         repeat
```

Alternative representations:

```
(.        for  [
.)        for  ]
@ or ^    for  ↑
```

Directives

```
forward
```

APPENDIX D

Syntax

An Extended Backus-Naur Form (EBNF) specification of the syntax of a programming language consists of a collection of rules or productions collectively called a "grammar" that describe the formation of sentences in the language. Each production consists of a non-terminal symbol and an EBNF expression separated by an equal sign and terminated with a period. The non-terminal symbol is a "meta-identifier" (a syntactic constant denoted by an English word), and the EBNF expression is its definition.

The EBNF expression is composed of zero or more terminal symbols, non-terminal symbols, and other metasymbols summarized in the table below:

Metasymbol	Meaning
=	is defined to be
|	alternatively
.	end of production
[X]	0 or 1 instance of X
{X}	0 or more instances of X
(X | Y)	a grouping: either X or Y
"XYZ"	the terminal symbol XYZ
MetaIdentifier	the non-terminal symbol *MetaIdentifier*

As an example, EBNF can be used to define its own syntax.

Syntax   = { *Production* } .
Production = *NonTerminal* "=" *Expression* "." .
Expression = *Term* { "|" *Term* } .
Term   = *Factor* { *Factor* } .
Factor   = *NonTerminal* | *Terminal* | "(" *Expression* ")" |
                "[" *Expression* "]" | "{" *Expression* "}" .
Terminal   = """" *Character* { *Character* } """" .
NonTerminal = *Letter* { *Letter* | *Digit* } .

Notes:

1.   A terminal symbol (literal) is always enclosed in quotation marks ('); if a " itself is enclosed, it is written twice. Thus in the Pascal EBNF below "["and "]" represent left and right brackets in a Pascal program, whereas [and] are meta-symbols in an EBNF expression that specify zero or one occurrence of whatever they enclose.

2.   Every syntax has a *start symbol*, a meta-identifier from which all the sentences in the language are generated. The start symbol for the Pascal syntax is *Program*.

Collected EBNF, Hierarchical

```
 1  Program              = ProgramHeading ";" Block "." .
 2  ProgramHeading       = "program" Identifier [ ProgramParameterList ] .
 3  ProgramParameterList = "(" IdentifierList ")" .
 4
 5  --------------------
 6
 7  Block                = LabelDeclarationPart
 8                         ConstantDefinitionPart
 9                         TypeDefinitionPart
10                         VariableDeclarationPart
11                         ProcedureAndFunctionDeclarationPart
12                         StatementPart .
13  LabelDeclarationPart = [ "label" DigitSequence { "," DigitSequence } ";" ] .
14  ConstantDefinitionPart = [ "const" ConstantDefinition ";"
15                           { ConstantDefinition ";" } ] .
16  TypeDefinitionPart   = [ "type" TypeDefinition ";"
17                           { TypeDefinition ";" } ] .
18  VariableDeclarationPart= [ "var" VariableDeclaration ";"
19                           { VariableDeclaration ";" } ] .
20  ProcedureAndFunctionDeclarationPart =
21                         { (ProcedureDeclaration | FunctionDeclaration) ";" }.
22  StatementPart        = CompoundStatement .
23
24  --------------------
25
26  ConstantDefinition   = Identifier "=" Constant .
27  TypeDefinition       = Identifier "=" Type .
28  VariableDeclaration  = IdentifierList ":" Type .
29  ProcedureDeclaration = ProcedureHeading ";" Block |
30                         ProcedureHeading ";" Directive |
31                         ProcedureIdentification ";" Block .
```

```
32 FunctionDeclaration      = FunctionHeading ";" Block |
33                            FunctionHeading ";" Directive |
34                            FunctionIdentification ";" Block .
35
36 ----------------------
37
38 ProcedureHeading         = "procedure" Identifier [ FormalParameterList ] .
39 ProcedureIdentification  = "procedure" ProcedureIdentifier .
40 FunctionHeading          = "function" Identifier [ FormalParameterList ]
41                            ":" ResultType .
42 FunctionIdentification   = "function" FunctionIdentifier .
43 FormalParameterList      = "(" FormalParameterSection
44                            { ";" FormalParameterSection } ")" .
45 FormalParameterSection   = ValueParameterSpecification |
46                            VariableParameterSpecification |
47                            ProceduralParameterSpecification |
48                            FunctionalParameterSpecification .
49
50 ----------------------
51
52 ValueParameterSpecification =
53                            IdentifierList ":" ( TypeIdentifier |
54                            ConformantArraySchema ) .
55 VariableParameterSpecification =
56                            "var" IdentifierList ":" ( TypeIdentifier |
57                            ConformantArraySchema ) .
58 ProceduralParameterSpecification =
59                            ProcedureHeading .
60 FunctionalParameterSpecification =
61                            FunctionHeading .
62 ConformantArraySchema = PackedConformantArraySchema |
63                            UnpackedConformantArraySchema .
64 PackedConformantArraySchema =
65                            "packed" "array" "[" IndexTypeSpecification "]" "of"
66                            TypeIdentifier .
67 UnpackedConformantArraySchema =
68                            "array" "[" IndexTypeSpecification { ";"
69                            IndexTypeSpecification } "]" "of"
70                            ( TypeIdentifier | ConformantArraySchema ) .
71 IndexTypeSpecification   = Identifier ".." Identifier ":" OrdinalTypeIdentifier .
72
73 ----------------------
74
75 CompoundStatement        = "begin"
76                            StatementSequence
```

```
77                              "end" .
78   StatementSequence      = Statement { ";" Statement } .
79   Statement              = [ Label ":" ]
80                              ( SimpleStatement | StructuredStatement ) .
81   SimpleStatement        = EmptyStatement | AssignmentStatement |
82                              ProcedureStatement | GotoStatement .
83   StructuredStatement    = CompoundStatement | ConditionalStatement
84                              RepetitiveStatement | WithStatement .
85   ConditionalStatement   = IfStatement | CaseStatement .
86   RepetitiveStatement    = WhileStatement | RepeatStatement | ForStatement .
87
88   ---------------------
89
90   EmptyStatement         = .
91   AssignmentStatement    = ( Variable | FunctionIdentifier ) ":=" Expression .
92   ProcedureStatement     = ProcedureIdentifier [ ActualParameterList |
93                              WriteParameterList ] .
94   GotoStatement          = "goto" Label .
95   IfStatement            = "if" BooleanExpression "then" Statement
96                              [ "else" Statement ] .
97   CaseStatement          = "case" CaseIndex "of"
98                              Case { ";" Case } [ ";" ]
99                              "end" .
100  RepeatStatement        = "repeat"
101                              StatementSequence
102                              "until" BooleanExpression .
103  WhileStatement         = "while" BooleanExpression "do"
104                              Statement .
105  ForStatement           = "for" ControlVariable ":=" InitialValue
106                              ( "to" | "downto" ) FinalValue "do" Statement .
107  WithStatement          = "with" RecordVariableList "do"
108                              Statement .
109  RecordVariableList     = RecordVariable { "," RecordVariable } .
110  CaseIndex              = OrdinalExpression .
111  Case                   = Constant { "," Constant } ":" Statement .
112  ControlVariable        = VariableIdentifier .
113  InitialValue           = OrdinalExpression .
114  FinalValue             = OrdinalExpression .
115
116  ---------------------
117
118  Type                   = SimpleType | StructuredType | PointerType .
119  SimpleType             = OrdinalType | RealTypeIdentifier .
120  StructuredType         = [ "packed" ] UnpackedStructuredType |
121                              StructuredTypeIdentifier .
```

122	*PointerType*	=	*"↑" DomainType* | *PointerTypeIdentifier* .
123	*OrdinalType*	=	*EnumeratedType* | *SubrangeType* |
124			*OrdinalTypeIdentifier* .
125	*UnpackedStructuredType*	=	*ArrayType* | *RecordType* | *SetType* | *FileType* .
126	*DomainType*	=	*TypeIdentifier* .
127	*EnumeratedType*	=	*"(" IdentifierList ")"* .
128	*SubrangeType*	=	*Constant ".." Constant* .
129			
130			
131	*ArrayType*	=	*"array" "[" IndexType* { *"," IndexType* } *"]" "of"*
132			*ComponentType* .
133	*RecordType*	=	*"record"*
134			*FieldList*
135			*"end"* .
136	*SetType*	=	*"set" "of" BaseType* .
137	*FileType*	=	*"file" "of" ComponentType* .
138	*IndexType*	=	*OrdinalType* .
139	*ComponentType*	=	*Type* .
140	*BaseType*	=	*OrdinalType* .
141	*ResultType*	=	*OrdinalTypeIdentifier* | *RealTypeIdentifier* |
142			*PointerTypeIdentifier* .
143	*FieldList*	=	[(*FixedPart* [*";" VariantPart*] | *VariantPart*)
144			[*";"*]] .
145	*FixedPart*	=	*RecordSection* { *";" RecordSection* } .
146	*VariantPart*	=	*"case" VariantSelector "of"*
147			*Variant*
148			{ *";" Variant* } .
149	*RecordSection*	=	*IdentifierList ":" Type* .
150	*VariantSelector*	=	[*TagField ":"*] *TagType* .
151	*Variant*	=	*Constant* { *"," Constant* } *":" "(" FieldList ")"* .
152	*TagType*	=	*OrdinalTypeIdentifier* .
153	*TagField*	=	*Identifier* .
154			
155	- - - - - - - - - - - - - - - - - - - -		
156			
157	*Constant*	=	[*Sign*] (*UnsignedNumber* | *ConstantIdentifier*) |
158			*CharacterString* .
159			
160	- - - - - - - - - - - - - - - - - - - -		
161			
162	*Expression*	=	*SimpleExpression* [*RelationalOperator*
163			*SimpleExpression*] .
164	*SimpleExpression*	=	[*Sign*] *Term* { *AddingOperator Term* } .
165	*Term*	=	*Factor* { *MultiplyingOperator Factor* } .

166	*Factor*	= *UnsignedConstant* | *BoundIdentifier* | *Variable* |
167		*SetConstructor* | *FunctionDesignator* |
168		"not" *Factor* | "(" *Expression* ")" .
169	*RelationalOperator*	= "=" | "<>" | "<" | "<=" | ">" | ">=" | "in" .
170	*AddingOperator*	= "+" | "-" | "or" .
171	*MultiplyingOperator*	= "*" | "/" | "div" | "mod" | "and" .
172	*UnsignedConstant*	= *UnsignedNumber* | *CharacterString* |
173		*ConstantIdentifier* | "nil" .
174	*FunctionDesignator*	= *FunctionIdentifier* [*ActualParameterList*] .
175		
176	- - - - - - - - - - - - - - - - - - - -	
177		
178	*Variable*	= *EntireVariable* | *ComponentVariable* |
179		*IdentifiedVariable* | *BufferVariable* .
180	*EntireVariable*	= *VariableIdentifier* .
181	*ComponentVariable*	= *IndexedVariable* | *FieldDesignator* .
182	*IdentifiedVariable*	= *PointerVariable* "↑" .
183	*BufferVariable*	= *FileVariable* "↑" .
184	*IndexedVariable*	= *ArrayVariable* "[" *Index* { "," *Index* } "]" .
185	*FieldDesignator*	= [*RecordVariable* "."] *FieldIdentifier* .
186	*SetConstructor*	= "[" [*ElementDescription* {"," *ElementDescription*}]"]".
187	*ElementDescription*	= *OrdinalExpression* [".." *OrdinalExpression*] .
188	*ActualParameterList*	= "(" *ActualParameter* { "," *ActualParameter* } ")" .
189	*ActualParameter*	= *Expression* | *Variable* | *ProcedureIdentifier* |
190		*FunctionIdentifier* .
191	*WriteParameterList*	= "(" (*FileVariable* | *WriteParameter*)
192		{ "," *WriteParameter* } ")" .
193	*WriteParameter*	= *Expression* [":" *IntegerExpression*
194		[":" *IntegerExpression*]] .
195	*ArrayVariable*	= *Variable* .
196	*RecordVariable*	= *Variable* .
197	*FileVariable*	= *Variable* .
198	*PointerVariable*	= *Variable* .
199	*IntegerExpression*	= *OrdinalExpression* .
200	*BooleanExpression*	= *OrdinalExpression* .
201	*OrdinalExpression*	= *Expression* .
202		
203	- - - - - - - - - - - - - - - - - - - -	
204		
205	*PointerTypeIdentifier*	= *TypeIdentifier* .
206	*StructuredTypeIdentifier*	= *TypeIdentifier* .
207	*OrdinalTypeIdentifier*	= *TypeIdentifier* .
208	*RealTypeIdentifier*	= *TypeIdentifier* .
209	*ConstantIdentifier*	= *Identifier* .

210	*TypeIdentifier*	= *Identifier* .
211	*VariableIdentifier*	= *Identifier* .
212	*FieldIdentifier*	= *Identifier* .
213	*ProcedureIdentifier*	= *Identifier* .
214	*FunctionIdentifier*	= *Identifier* .
215	*BoundIdentifier*	= *Identifier* .
216		
217		
218	*UnsignedNumber*	= *UnsignedInteger* │ *UnsignedReal* .
219	*IdentifierList*	= *Identifier* ["," *Identifier*] .
220		
221	----------------------	
222		
223	*Identifier*	= *Letter* [*Letter* │ *Digit*] .
224	*Directive*	= *Letter* [*Letter* │ *Digit*] .
225	*Label*	= *DigitSequence* .
226	*UnsignedInteger*	= *DigitSequence* .
227	*UnsignedReal*	= *UnsignedInteger* "." *DigitSequence*["e" *ScaleFactor*]│
228		*UnsignedInteger* "e" *ScaleFactor* .
229	*ScaleFactor*	= [*Sign*] *UnsignedInteger* .
230	*Sign*	= "+" │ "−" .
231	*CharacterString*	= "'" *StringElement* { *StringElement* } "'" .
232	*DigitSequence*	= *Digit* { *Digit* } .
233		
234	*Letter*	= "a" │ "b" │ "c" │ "d" │ "e" │ "f" │ "g" │
235		"h" │ "i" │ "j" │ "k" │ "l" │ "m" │ "n" │
236		"o" │ "p" │ "q" │ "r" │ "s" │ "t" │ "s" │
237		"v" │ "w" │ "x" │ "y" │ "z" .
238	*Digit*	= "0" │ "1" │ "2" │ "3" │ "4" │ "5" │ "6" │
239		"7" │ "8" │ "9" .
240	*StringElement*	= "''" │ *AnyCharacterExceptApostrophe* .

Cross Reference of EBNF Indexed to Report

Report	Meta-Identifier/Word Symbol	EBNF Cross Reference
11.3.2.	*ActualParameter*	188 188 189
11.3.2.	*ActualParameterList*	92 174 188
8.	*AddingOperator*	164 170
4.	*AnyCharacterExceptApostrophe*	240
6.2.1.	*ArrayType*	125 131
7.2.1.	*ArrayVariable*	184 195
9.1.1.	*AssignmentStatement*	81 91
6.2.3.	*BaseType*	136 140
10.1.	*Block*	1 7 29 31 32 34
8.	*BooleanExpression*	95 102 103 200
11.3.1.1.	*BoundIdentifier*	166 215
7.4.	*BufferVariable*	179 183
9.2.2.2.	*Case*	98 98 111
9.2.2.2.	*CaseIndex*	97 110
9.2.2.2.	*CaseStatement*	85 97
4.	*CharacterString*	158 172 231
6.2.1.	*ComponentType*	132 137 139
7.2.	*ComponentVariable*	178 181
9.2.1.	*CompoundStatement*	22 75 83
9.2.2.	*ConditionalStatement*	83 85
11.3.1.1.	*ConformantArraySchema*	54 57 62 70
5.	*Constant*	26 111 111 128 151 151 157
5.	*ConstantDefinition*	14 15 26
5.	*ConstantDefinitionPart*	8 14
5.	*ConstantIdentifier*	157 173 209
9.2.3.3.	*ControlVariable*	105 112
4.	*Digit*	223 224 232 232 238
4.	*DigitSequence*	13 13 225 226 227 232
4.	*Directive*	30 33 224

Collected EBNF, Alphabetical

ActualParameter	=	*Expression* | *Variable* | *ProcedureIdentifier* | *FunctionIdentifier* .
ActualParameterList	=	"(" *ActualParameter* { "," *ActualParameter* } ")" .
AddingOperator	=	"+" | "-" | "or" .
ArrayType	=	"array" "[" *IndexType* { "," *IndexType* } "]" "of" *ComponentType* .
ArrayVariable	=	*Variable* .
AssignmentStatement	=	(*Variable* | *FunctionIdentifier*) ":=" *Expression* .
BaseType	=	*OrdinalType* .
Block	=	*LabelDeclarationPart* *ConstantDefinitionPart* *TypeDefinitionPart* *VariableDeclarationPart* *StatementPart* .
BooleanExpression	=	*OrdinalExpression* .
BoundIdentifier	=	*Identifier* .
BufferVariable	=	*FileVariable* "↑" .
Case	=	*Constant* { "," *Constant* } ":" *Statement* .
CaseIndex	=	*OrdinalExpression* .
CaseStatement	=	"case" *CaseIndex* "of" *Case* { ";" *Case* } [";"] "end" .
CharacterString	=	"'" *StringElement* { *StringElement* } "'" .
ComponentType	=	*Type* .
ComponentVariable	=	*IndexedVariable* | *FieldDesignator* .
CompoundStatement	=	"begin" *StatementSequence* "end" .
ConditionalStatement	=	*IfStatement* | *CaseStatement* .
ConformantArraySchema	=	*PackedConformantArraySchema* | *UnpackedConformantArraySchema* .
Constant	=	[*Sign*] (*UnsignedNumber* | *ConstantIdentifier*) | *CharacterString* .
ConstantDefinition	=	*Identifier* "=" *Constant* .

225

ConstantDefinitionPart   = ["const" *ConstantDefinition* ";"
                                    { *ConstantDefinition* ";" }] .
ConstantIdentifier   = *Identifier* .
ControlVariable   = *VariableIdentifier* .
Digit   = "0" | "1" | "2" | "3" | "4" | "5" | "6" |
                                "7" | "8" | "9" .
DigitSequence   = *Digit* { *Digit* } .
Directive   = *Letter* { *Letter* | *Digit* } .
DomainType   = *TypeIdentifier* .
ElementDescription   = *OrdinalExpression* [".." *OrdinalExpression*] .
EmptyStatement   = .
EntireVariable   = *VariableIdentifier* .
EnumeratedType   = "(" *IdentifierList* ")" .
Expression   = *SimpleExpression* [*RelationalOperator*
                                    SimpleExpression] .
Factor   = *UnsignedConstant* | *BoundIdentifier* | *Variable* |
                                    SetConstructor | *FunctionDesignator* |
                                    "not" *Factor* | "(" *Expression* ")" .
FieldDesignator   = [*RecordVariable* "."] *FieldIdentifier* .
FieldIdentifier   = *Identifier* .
FieldList   = [(*FixedPart* [";" *VariantPart*] |
                                    VariantPart)] | [";"]] .
FileType   = "file" "of" *ComponentType* .
FileVariable   = *Variable* .
FinalValue   = *OrdinalExpression* .
FixedPart   = *RecordSection* { ";" *RecordSection* } .
ForStatement   = "for" *ControlVariable* ":=" *InitialValue*
                                    ("to" | "downto") *FinalValue* "do" *Statement* .
FormalParameterList   = "(" *FormalParameterSection*
                                    { ";" *FormalParameterSection* } ")" .
FormalParameterSection   = *ValueParameterSpecification* |
                                    VariableParameterSpecification |
                                    ProceduralParameterSpecification |
                                    FunctionalParameterSpecification .
FunctionDeclaration   = *FunctionHeading* ";" *Block* |
                                    FunctionHeading ";" *Directive* |
                                    FunctionIdentification ";" *Block* .
FunctionDesignator   = *FunctionIdentifier* [*ActualParameterList*] .
FunctionHeading   = "function" *Identifier* [*FormalParameterList*]
                                    ":" *ResultType* .
FunctionIdentification   = "function" *FunctionIdentifier* .
FunctionIdentifier   = *Identifier* .
FunctionalParameterSpecification =
                                FunctionHeading .
GotoStatement   = "goto" *Label* .
IdentifiedVariable   = *PointerVariable* "↑" .
Identifier   = *Letter* { *Letter* | *Digit* } .
IdentifierList   = *Identifier* { "," *Identifier* } .

IfStatement	=	"if" *BooleanExpression* "then" *Statement* ["else" *Statement*] .
IndexType	=	*OrdinalType* .
IndexTypeSpecification	=	*Identifier* ".." *Identifier* ":" *OrdinalTypeIdentifier* .
IndexedVariable	=	*ArrayVariable* "[" *Index* { "," *Index* } "]" .
InitialValue	=	*OrdinalExpression* .
IntegerExpression	=	*OrdinalExpression* .
Label	=	*DigitSequence* .
LabelDeclarationPart	=	["label" *DigitSequence* { "," *DigitSequence* } ";"] .
Letter	=	"a" │ "b" │ "c" │ "d" │ "e" │ "f" │ "g" │ "h" │ "i" │ "j" │ "k" │ "l" │ "m" │ "n" │ "o" │ "p" │ "q" │ "r" │ "s" │ "t" │ "u" │ "v" │ "w" │ "x" │ "y" │ "z" .
MultiplyingOperator	=	"*" │ "/" │ "div" │ "mod" │ "and" .
OrdinalExpression	=	*Expression* .
OrdinalType	=	*EnumeratedType* │ *SubrangeType* │ *OrdinalTypeIdentifier* .
OrdinalTypeIdentifier	=	*TypeIdentifier* .
PackedConformantArraySchema	=	
		"packed" "array" "[" *IndexTypeSpecification* "]" "of" *TypeIdentifier* .
PointerType	=	"↑" *DomainType* │ *PointerTypeIdentifier* .
PointerTypeIdentifier	=	*TypeIdentifier* .
PointerVariable	=	*Variable* .
ProceduralParameterSpecification	=	
		ProcedureHeading .
ProcedureAndFunctionDeclarationPart	=	
		{ (*ProcedureDeclaration* │ *FunctionDeclaration*) ";" }.
ProcedureDeclaration	=	*ProcedureHeading* ";" *Block* │ *ProcedureHeading* ";" *Directive* │ *ProcedureIdentification* ";" *Block* .
ProcedureHeading	=	"procedure" *Identifier* [*FormalParameterList*] .
ProcedureIdentification	=	"procedure" *ProcedureIdentifier* .
ProcedureIdentifier	=	*Identifier* .
ProcedureStatement	=	*ProcedureIdentifier* [*ActualParameterList* │ *WriteParameterList*] .
Program	=	*ProgramHeading* ";" *Block* "." .
ProgramHeading	=	"program" *Identifier* [*ProgramParameterList*] .
ProgramParameterList	=	"(" *IdentifierList* ")" .
RealTypeIdentifier	=	*TypeIdentifier* .
RecordSection	=	*IdentifierList* ":" *Type* .
RecordType	=	"record" *FieldList* "end" .
RecordVariable	=	*Variable* .
RecordVariableList	=	*RecordVariable* { "," *RecordVariable* } .
RelationalOperator	=	"=" │ "<>" │ "<" │ "<=" │ ">" │ ">=" │ "in".
RepeatStatement	=	"repeat"

		StatementSequence "until" *BooleanExpression* .
RepetitiveStatement	=	*WhileStatement* | *RepeatStatement* | *ForStatement.*
ResultType	=	*OrdinalTypeIdentifier* | *RealTypeIdentifier* | *PointerTypeIdentifier* .
ScaleFactor	=	[*Sign*] *UnsignedInteger* .
SetConstructor	=	"[" [*ElementDescription* { "," *ElementDescription*}] "]".
SetType	=	"set" "of" *BaseType* .
Sign	=	"+" | "-" .
SimpleExpression	=	[*Sign*] *Term* { *AddingOperator Term* } .
SimpleStatement	=	*EmptyStatement* | *AssignmentStatement* | *ProcedureStatement* | *GotoStatement* .
SimpleType	=	*OrdinalType* | *RealTypeIdentifier* .
Statement	=	[*Label* ":"] (*SimpleStatement* | *StructuredStatement*) .
StatementPart	=	*CompoundStatement* .
StatementSequence	=	*Statement* { ";" *Statement* } .
StringElement	=	"''" | *AnyCharacterExceptApostrophe* .
StructuredStatement	=	*CompoundStatement* | *ConditionalStatement* | *RepetitiveStatement* | *WithStatement* .
StructuredType	=	["packed"] *UnpackedStructuredType* | *StructuredTypeIdentifier* .
StructuredTypeIdentifier	=	*TypeIdentifier* .
SubrangeType	=	*Constant* ".." *Constant* .
TagField	=	*Identifier* .
TagType	=	*OrdinalTypeIdentifier* .
Term	=	*Factor* { *MultiplyingOperator Factor* } .
Type	=	*SimpleType* | *StructuredType* | *PointerType* .
TypeDefinition	=	*Identifier* "=" *Type* .
TypeDefinitionPart	=	["type" *TypeDefinition* ";" { *TypeDefinition* ";" }] .
TypeIdentifier	=	*Identifier* .
UnpackedConformantArraySchema	=	
		"array" "[" *IndexTypeSpecification* } ";" *IndexTypeSpecification* } "]" "of" (*TypeIdentifier* | *ConformantArraySchema*) .
UnpackedStructuredType	=	*ArrayType* | *RecordType* | *SetType* | *FileType* .
UnsignedConstant	=	*UnsignedNumber* | *CharacterString* | *ConstantIdentifier* | "nil" .
UnsignedInteger	=	*DigitSequence* .
UnsignedNumber	=	*UnsignedInteger* | *UnsignedReal* .
UnsignedReal	=	*UnsignedInteger* "." *DigitSequence* ["e" *ScaleFactor*]| *UnsignedInteger* "e" *ScaleFactor* .
ValueParameterSpecification	=	
		IdentifierList ":" (*TypeIdentifier* | *ConformantArraySchema*) .
Variable	=	*EntireVariable* | *ComponentVariable* | *IdentifiedVariable* | *BufferVariable* .

```
VariableDeclaration          =  IdentifierList ":" Type .
VariableDeclarationPart      =  [ "var" VariableDeclaration ";"
                                      { VariableDeclaration ";" } ]  .
VariableIdentifier           =  Identifier .
VariableParameterSpecification =
                                "var" IdentifierList ":" ( TypeIdentifier  |
                                      ConformantArraySchema ) .
Variant                      =  Constant { "," Constant } ":" "(" FieldList ")" .
VariantPart                  =  "case" VariantSelector "of"
                                Variant
                                { ";" Variant } .
VariantSelector              =  [ TagField ":" ] TagType .
WhileStatement               =  "while" BooleanExpression "do"
                                Statement .
WithStatement                =  "with" RecordVariableList "do"
                                Statement .
WriteParameter               =  Expression [ ":" IntegerExpression
                                [ ":" IntegerExpression ] ]  .
WriteParameterList           =  "(" ( FileVariable  |  WriteParameter )
                                { "," WriteParameter } ")" .
```

Syntax Diagrams

The diagrams for *Letter*, *Digit*, *Identifier*, *Directive*, *UnsignedInteger*, *Unsigned-Number*, and *CharacterString* describe the formation of lexical symbols from characters. The other diagrams describe the formation of syntactic constructs from symbols.

Letter

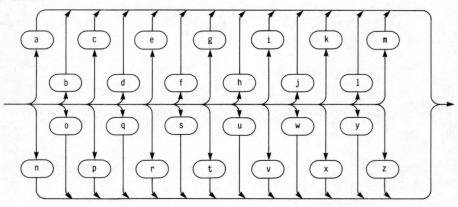

Digit

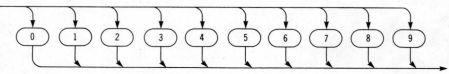

Identifier and Directive

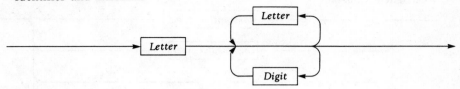

Unsigned Integer

UnsignedNumber

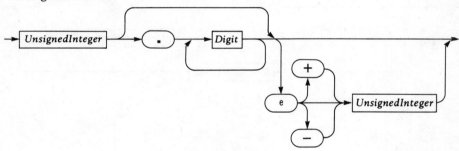

CharacterString

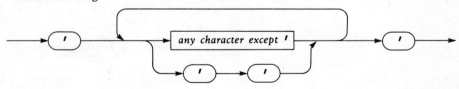

ConstantIdentifier, VariableIdentifier, FieldIdentifier, BoundIdentifier,
TypeIdentifier, ProcedureIdentifier and FunctionIdentifier

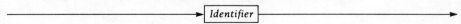

Unsigned Constant

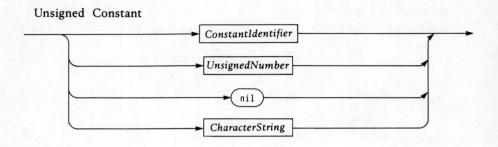

Constant

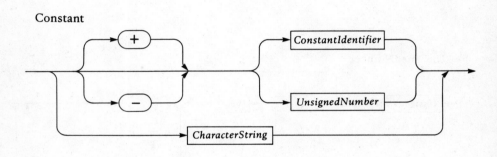

Variable

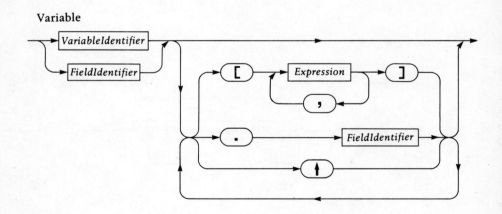

Factor

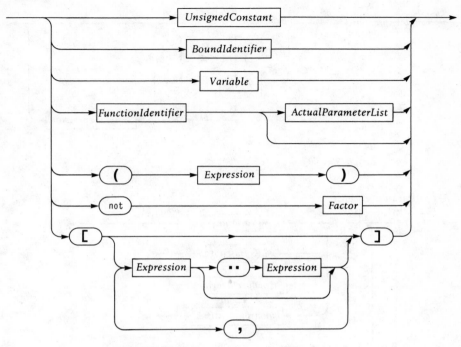

Term

SimpleExpression

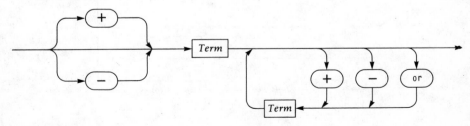

Expression

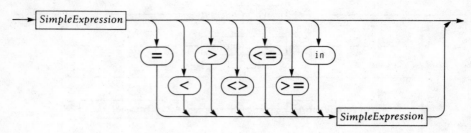

ActualParameterList

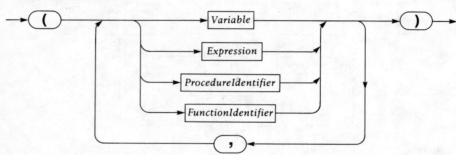

WriteParameterList

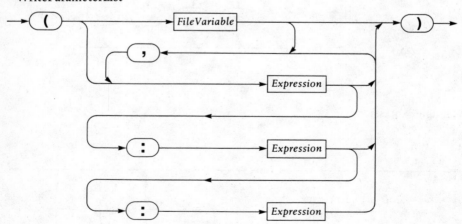

IndexTypeSpecification

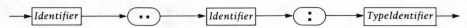

ConformantArraySchema

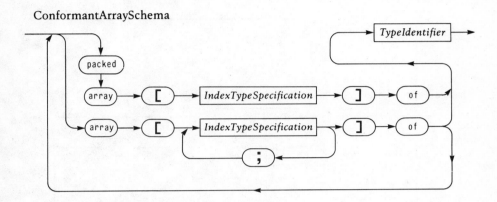

FormalParameterList

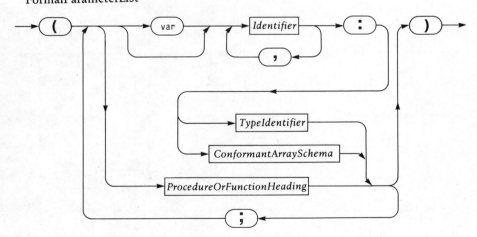

ProcedureOrFunctionHeading

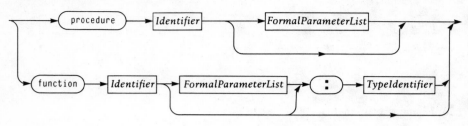

OrdinalType

Type

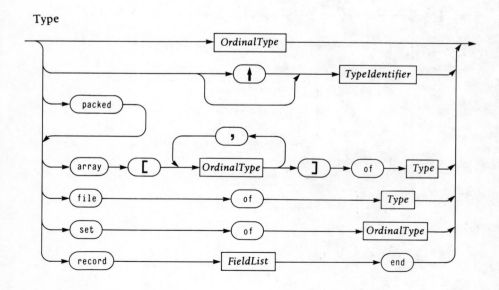

FieldList

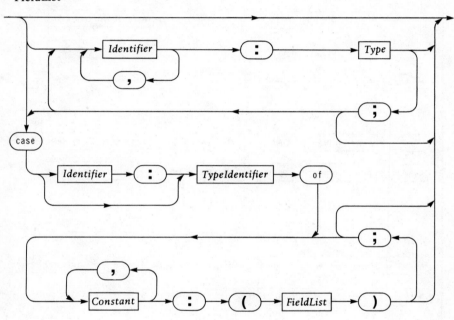

Statement

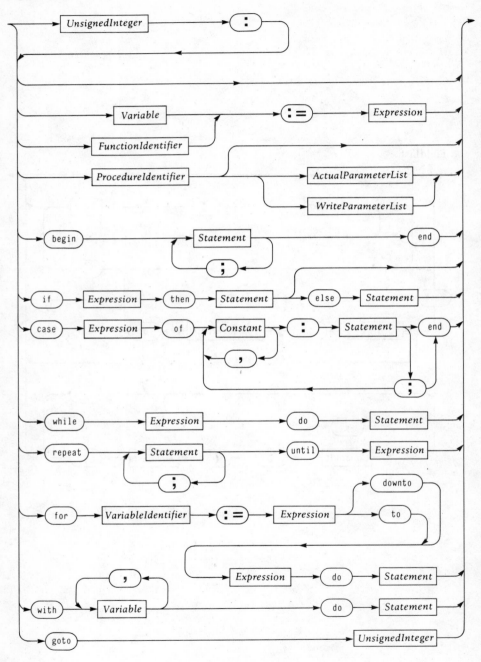

Block

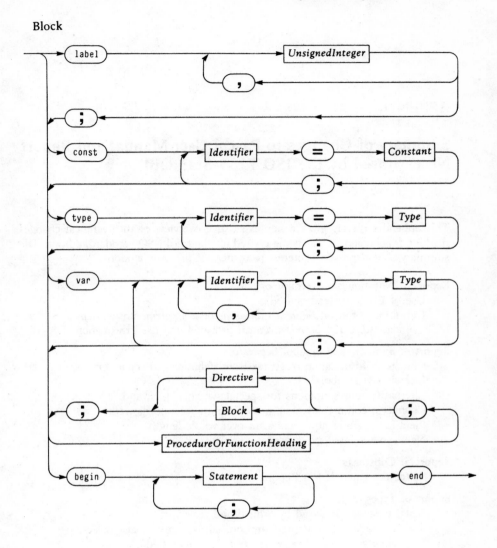

Program

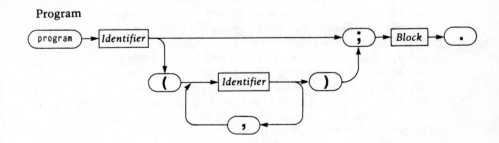

APPENDIX E

Summary of Changes to Pascal User Manual and Report Necessitated by the ISO 7185 Standard

This appendix merely gives a non-exhaustive overview of the technical changes made to this book as it was being revised for the third (ISO Standard) edition. The summary should prove of interest to owners of previous editions.

Report 3: Notation and Terminology
Use of EBNF instead of BNF.
Definitions of *error, implementation-defined, implementation-dependent, extension,* and *Standard Pascal* provided and used throughout Report.

Report 4: Symbols and Symbol Separators
Change in formulation of syntax from delimiters to separators.
Inclusion of symbol ".. ".
Alternative representations for special symbols "[,]", and "↑".
Change in comment syntax; nested comments not allowed.
Identifier spelling now significant over whole length.
New symbol category: directives.

Report 5: Constants
MaxInt now included in Report

Report 6: Types
Scalar types are replaced by ordinal and real types;
definitions of succ, pred, and ord, array indexing case selection,
subranges, and set base types thereby simplified.
Type compatibility now defined as "name compatibility."
Concepts of *assignment compatibility* and *assignable types* introduced.
Specific semantic implications for packed structured types.
Optional ";" allowed to complete syntax of record types.
Case labels in record variants now called case constants.
Full specification of variant parts required in record types.
Inspection and generation modes specified for file types.
Type text no longer equivalent to (packed) file of char.
File types or types containing file types (i.e., non-assignable types)
not allowed as component types of file types.
Domain types introduced for pointer types.

Report 7: Variables

Concept of *undefined* and *totally undefined* variables introduced.

Input and Output now implicitly declared, textfile, program parameters
   if used.

Report 8: Expressions

Factor now includes conformant-array parameter bound identifier.

Order of evaluation of expressions specified as implementation-dependent.

Definition of mod operator changed.

Type of a set constructor now both packed and unpacked.

Report 9: Statements

Rules enforced regarding the accessibility of labels by gotos.

Case statement labels now called case constants.

The control variable of a for statement now a local variable only.

Several restrictions added to the for statement and its actions
   rigorously defined.

Report 10: Blocks, Scope, and Activations

The concepts of a *program-point, activation-point, scope of the definition
   or declaration (introduction)* of labels and identifiers defined.

Scope rules defined precisely to eliminate ambiguity.

The apparent integral value of labels greater than 9999 not allowed.

Report 11: Procedures and Functions

Procedure and function directives are introduced;
   forward now a standard directive.

Conformant-array parameters added; the concept of *conformability*
   and conformant type introduced.

Full specification of the parameter lists now required of formal
   procedural and functional parameters (procedures and functions
   as parameters); the concept of *parameter-list congruency* introduced.

Use of tag fields as actual variable parameters disallowed.

Specification of the array parameters to pack and unpack changed.

File-handling procedures and functions and the state of the file variable
   and buffer variable now rigorously defined.

Report 12: Textfile Input and Output

Procedure page standard; its file parameter optional;
   its actions changed.

Special *WriteParameterList* syntax added as actual parameter lists to
   write and writeln.

Field widths in formatted write and writeln procedures now precisely
   defined.

Report 13: Programs

Program parameters now optional and their nature specified.

Report 14: Compliance with ISO 7185

Definitions of *complying program* and *complying processor* given.

Requirements for compliance with the ISO Pascal Standard explained.

APPENDIX F

Programming Examples

Two examples are presented: a program is developed as an illustration of the method of stepwise refinement [see Reference 2] followed by a procedure serving as a model of portable software.

Example 1: `Program IsItAPalindrome`

A program is developed to find all integers from 1 to 100 whose squares are palindromes. For example: 11 squared is 121 which is a palindrome.

A palindrome is a string of symbols from an alphabet which reads the same in forward or reverse order. Well-known examples in English include (ignoring blanks and punctuation):

"radar"
"a man, a plan, a canal, Panama"
"Doc, note, I dissent! A fast never prevents a fatness; I diet on cod."

Example 1 Step 1:

```
program IsItAPalindrome(Output);

begin
   FindAllIntegersFrom1To100WhoseSquaresArePalindromes
end { IsItAPalindrome } .
```

Example 1 Step 2:

```
program IsItAPalindrome(Output);

   { Find all integers from 1 to 100 whose squares are palindromes. }
```

```
const
    Maximum = 100;

type
    IntRange = 1..Maximum;

var
    N: IntRange;

begin
    for N := 1 to Maximum do
        if Palindrome(Sqr(N)) then
            Writeln(N, ' squared is a palindrome.')
end { IsItAPalindrome } .
```

Example 1   Step 3:

```
program IsItAPalindrome(Output);

    { Find all integers from 1 to 100 whose squares are palindromes. }

    const
        Maximum = 100;

    type
        IntRange = 1..Maximum;

    var
        N: IntRange;

    function Palindrome(Square: Integer): Boolean;

        var
            NPlaces = 1..5 { 5 = Log10(Sqr(Maximum)) + 1 };

    begin { Palindrome }
        CrackDigits;
        Palindrome := CheckSymmetry(1, NPlaces)
    end { Palindrome };

begin
    for N := 1 to Maximum do
        if Palindrome(Sqr(N)) then
            Writeln(N, ' squared is a palindrome.')
end { IsItAPalindrome } .
```

Example 1 Step 4:

```
program IsItAPalindrome(Output);

   { Find all integers from 1 to 100 whose squares are palindromes. }

   const
      Maximum = 100;

   type
      IntRange = 1..Maximum;

   var
      N: IntRange;

   function Palindrome(Square: Integer): Boolean;
   const
      Places = 5 { = Trunc(Log10(Sqr(Maximum))) + 1 };

   type
      NPlaces = 1..Places;
      SingleDigit = 0..9;
      DigitVec = array [NPlaces] of SingleDigit;

   var
      Digits: DigitVec;
      Size: NPlaces;

   procedure CrackDigits;
   begin
      Size := 1;
      while Square > 9 do
         begin
            Digits[Size] := Square mod 10;
            Square := Square div 10;
            Size := Size + 1
         end;
      Digits[Size] := Square
   end { CrackDigits };

   function CheckSymmetry(Left, Right: NPlaces): Boolean;
   begin
      if Left >= Right then CheckSymmetry := true
      else
         if Digits[Left] = Digits[Right] then
            CheckSymmetry := CheckSymmetry(Left + 1, Right - 1)
         else CheckSymmetry := false
   end { CheckSymmetry };
```

```
   begin { Palindrome }
      CrackDigits;
      Palindrome := CheckSymmetry(1, Size)
   end { Palindrome };

begin
   for N := 1 to Maximum do
      if Palindrome(Sqr(N)) then
         Writeln(N, ' squared is a palindrome.')
end { IsItAPalindrome } .
```

Example 2: Procedure ReadRadixRepresentation

A generalized procedure to read integers expressed in any radix from 2 to 16 is presented.

```
type Radix = 2..16;

procedure ReadRadixRepresentation
            (var F: Text;      { contains the representation }
             var E: Boolean;   { indicates presence of errors }
             var X: Integer;   { set to result if no errors occur }
                 R: Radix      { radix of representation }
            );

{ ReadRadixRepresentation assumes that textfile F is positioned
  to read a sequence of extended digits as a radix-R representation
  of an integer. The extended digits, in ascending order, are:

     '0','1','2','3','4','5','6','7','8','9','a','b','c','d','e','f'

  Upper-case letters corresponding to the lower-case letters
     may be used.
  The parameter E indicates whether one of the following errors
     occurred:
     (1)  The textfile F was not positioned to a sequence of
          extended digits.
     (2)  The sequence of digits represents an integer greater
          than Maxint.
     (3)  The sequence of extended digits contains a digit that
          is not a radix-R digit. }
```

```
type
   DigitRange = 0..15;

var
   D: DigitRange;
   V: Boolean;
   S: 0..Maxint;

procedure ConvertExtendedDigit(C: Char; var V: Boolean;
                                        var D: DigitRange);
   { ConvertExtendedDigit determines whether C is an extended
     digit, setting V to indicate its validity, and if V is
     true sets D to the numerical value of the extended digit. }

begin { ConvertExtendedDigit }
   V := C in [ '0'..'9','a','b','c','d','e','f',
                       'A','B','C','D','E','F' ];
   if V then
      case C of
         '0': D := 0;  '1': D := 1;  '2': D := 2;  '3': D := 3;
         '4': D := 4;  '5': D := 5;  '6': D := 6;  '7': D := 7;
         '8': D := 8;  '9': D := 9;
         'A','a': D := 10;  'B','b': D := 11;  'C','c': D := 12;
         'D','d': D := 13;  'E','e': D := 14'  'F','f': D := 15;
      end
end { ConvertExtendedDigit };

begin { ReadRadixRepresentation }
   E := true;
   ConvertExtendedDigit(F↑,V,D);
   if V then
      begin
         E := false;  S := 0;
         repeat
            if D < R then
               if (Maxint - D) div R >= S then
                  begin
                     S := S * R + D;
                     Get(F);
                     ConvertExtendedDigit(F↑,V,D);
                  end
               else E := true
            else E := true
         until E or not V;
         if not E then X := S
      end
end { ReadRadixRepresentation } .
```

APPENDIX G

The ASCII Character Set

ASCII (American Standard Code for Information Interchange) is the American variant of an officially-recognized standard, international character set called the ISO (International Organization for Standardization) set. It specifies an encoding for 128 characters. Within the ISO character code there may exist national variants for 12 symbols (such as the currency symbol $). The 128 characters consist of 95 which print as single graphics and 33 which are used for device control. The backspace control character is specifically used to allow overprinting of characters such as accents on letters in some languages.

the 33 control characters:

ACK	Acknowledge	FF	Form Feed
BEL	Bell	FS	File Separator
BS	Backspace	GS	Group Separator
CAN	Cancel	HT	Horizontal Tab
CR	Carriage Return	LF	Line Feed
DC1	Device Control 1	NAK	Negative Acknowledge
DC2	Device Control 2	NUL	Null
DC3	Device Control 3	RS	Record Separator
DC4	Device Control 4	SI	Shift In
DEL	Delete	SO	Shift Out
DLE	Data Link Escape	SOH	Start of Heading
EM	End of Medium	STX	Start of Text
ENQ	Enquiry	SUB	Substitute
EOT	End of Transmission	SYN	Synchronous Idle
ESC	Escape	US	Unit Separator
ETB	End of Transmission Block	VT	Vertical Tab
ETX	End of Text		

the full 128-character set:

	00	16	32	48	64	80	96	112
0	NUL	DLE		0	@	P	`	p
1	SOH	DC1	!	1	A	Q	a	q
2	STX	DC2	"	2	B	R	b	r
3	ETX	DC3	#	3	C	S	c	s
4	EOT	DC4	$	4	D	T	d	t
5	ENQ	NAK	%	5	E	U	e	u
6	ACK	SYN	&	6	F	V	f	v
7	BEL	ETB	'	7	G	W	g	w
8	BS	CAN	(	8	H	X	h	x
9	HT	EM	)	9	I	Y	i	y
10	LF	SUB	*	:	J	Z	j	z
11	VT	ESC	+	;	K	[	k	{
12	FF	FS	,	<	L	\	l		
13	CR	GS	-	=	M	]	m	}
14	SO	RS	.	>	N	^	n	~
15	SI	US	/	?	O	_	o	DEL

The 7-bit code for a character is the sum of the column and row numbers. For example, the code for the letter G is $7 + 64 = 71$.

Index to Programs,
Program Fragments, and Program Schemata

Index

Abs, 18, 20, 192, 204, 211
Absolute value, *see* Abs
Abstraction, 14
Action, concept of, 1, 28, 143
Activation
  and formal parameters, 185
  point, 171, 180, 186
Activations, 171, 177, 179–180
Active variant, of record, 70, 100,
    157, 191
Actual
  functional parameter, 122, 124, 188
  parameter, 106–107, 110, 111–113,
    146, 175, 180, 184, 185,
    186–187
    EBNF for, 187, 219, 225
    lists, 106, 107, 170, 186–188
      EBNF for, 187, 219, 225
      syntax diagram for, 107, 234
  procedural parameter, 117, 121,
    187–188
  value conformant array parameter,
    113, 187
  value parameter, 110, 187
  variable parameter, 110, 154, 175,
    187

Adding operators
  EBNF for, 164, 219, 225
  operands of, 165
  and precedence, 32, 166
  (*see also* Arithmetic operators)
Addresses, for pointer types, 94
Algol 60, vii, 6, 7, 8, 142–143
Algo-W, vii
Algorithm, 1, 179
Alternative representations, of sym-
    bols, 10, 148, 212
And, 16, 167, 208, 212 (*see also* Boo-
    lean operators)
Apostrophe, how to represent, 18, 150
Arabic to Roman, program for, 45–46
ArcTan, 20, 193, 204, 211
Arctangent, *see* ArcTan
Argument, *see* Parameter
Arithmetic
  functions, predeclared, 192–193
  operations, on Boolean values, 8
  operators, 17, 145, 166–167, 208
Array
  components of, 144, 155
  conformant, *see* Conformant array
  data types, 55, 210